GLOBAL IMMIGRATION CRISIS

Dick Sim

Global Immigration Crisis
Copyright © 2024 by Dick Sim

All rights reserved. No part of this book may be reproduced or transmitted in any form or by any means, electronic or mechanical, including photocopying, recording, or by any information storage and retrieval system without express written permission from the author, except in the case of brief quotations embodied in critical reviews and certain other noncommercial uses permitted by copyright law.

This is a work of nonfiction. No names have been changed, no characters invented, no events fabricated.

Printed in the United States of America.

ISBN
979-8-89376-134-4 (Paperback)
979-8-89376-135-1 (eBook)
979-8-89376-136-8 (Hardback)

Leap Write Literary
137 Forest Park Lane Thomasville
North Carolina 27360 USA

TABLE OF CONTENTS

Dick Sim v

Preview vii

Chapter 1.1 — Differences in Population Sizes and Growth Rates 1

Chapter 1.2 — Wealth Differences 10

Chapter 1.3 — Immigration- It is "Easy" 14

Chapter 2.1 — For God's Sake 20

Chapter 2.2 — Islam 25

Chapter 3.1 — How The USA Got Rich 29

Chapter 3.2 — How the Middle East Got Rich….Hint Oil 37

Chapter 3.3 — Hey- Let's Tax the Rich More 45

Chapter 4.1 — We The People Versus they the Government 48

Chapter 4.2 — Can Governments Respond? 66

Chapter 5 — The Four Thugs 68

Chapter 6 — The Human Reality 74

DICK SIM

Dick started life in Glasgow, Scotland. As a child he studied hard and played rugby at a unique private school founded in 1641. It worked. By age 23 he had a PhD in Engineering and was playing top level rugby as a "blue" at Cambridge University. In 1970 he emigrated to the US. He started as an engineer in the nuclear industry. By 1987 he was Chairman and CEO of a NYSE global industrial company. For about 30 years he ran companies that had employees of all races and religions all over the world. He has been exposed to many industries, technologies and cultures. In the last 20 years he has been a resident in the UK, Ireland, Italy and the US. Because of his diverse global background, he has a deep understanding of global capitalism, the development and purpose of technology and the conflicting human conditions around the world. Along the way he was presented to Queen Elizabeth, been a Visiting Professor at UC Berkley, and harvested his own olives in Italy. Today he is very active in supervising his farrier and blacksmith supplies business and is striving to be a better grandfather.

PREVIEW

This book covers many subjects that are topical today. It provides enough data, information, graphs and tables to try and give you the facts. It deals with the following topics:

- Increasing immigration pressures on Europe and the USA from Africa, the Middle East and Central America.
- The reality that very conservative Muslims cannot assimilate in Europe or the USA.
- That all countries in the world need to discuss and decide what they want their population to be in 2050. The choices are to be larger, about the same or smaller. The issues that guide that choice are many and complex but that is not an excuse to avoid debating them.
- Having benefited tremendously from free market capitalism, some in the USA are embracing socialism and getting lost. The best thing we can do for the poor is to reinvigorate our free market capitalistic heritage.
- We need a President that can confront and back down the bullies in charge of Russia, China, Iran and North Korea.
- We have lost our way culturally. The two parent, value driven home is endangered. We need to fix our selfish hedonistic culture and raise a generation of good persons who have the right values and the self-discipline to create a community worthy of our heritage.

CHAPTER 1.1

DIFFERENCES IN POPULATION SIZES AND GROWTH RATES

The global population is currently about 8 billion and it is expected to reach a peak of about 10 billion sometime in the latter half of this century. Included here are projections for the major geographical regions which show that Africa more than doubles in size while all the other regions are either flat or see modest declines.

Population projections (in millions) by continent from 2025 to 2100.

	2025	2050	2075	2100
Africa	1512	2465	3346	3917
L. Amer. & Caribbean	672	748	728	649
N. America	382	421	439	447
Asia	4800	5290	5147	4684
Europe	741	704	636	587
Oceania	46	57	64	68
World	8155	9687	10365	10355

https://www.ined.fr/en/everything_about_population/data/world-projections/projections-by- continent/

The empirical evidence is that fertility rates decline as income per capita increases. See correlation below.

Significant factors effecting population trends are;

1. The oral birth control pill became increasingly available starting in the 1960's and it is now readily available everywhere except Africa where there are less community health services.

2. Many women today are highly educated and making good money working. The balance between working and childcare is much different today as compared to 70 years ago. In Africa most women have yet to have this choice to make.
3. The adult time and the money to raise a child today is significantly more than 70 years ago. Back then kids were free range. Free range means that they could go to and from school by themselves. They could go out and play with other neighborhood kids with no adult involvement. They could be latch key kids which means they could do all these things when their parents were not yet home from work. Today this way of life no longer is possible in most families

A fertility rate of 2.1 is needed to maintain a population. The graph shows all regions of the world being below this number by 2030 except for Africa.

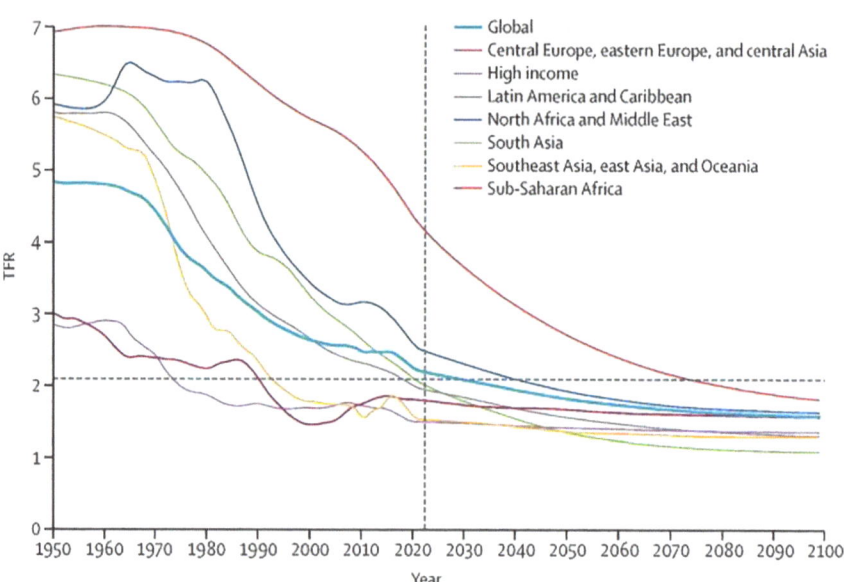

Figure 1. Total Fertility Rate, globally and by major regions, 1950–2100 from the lancet.com

Although it seems highly probable that the world population will peak, what is less certain is what happens then? Does it then decline and if it does will it stabilize at some lower level?

Already the native populations of Japan, South Korea and China are starting to decline. So perhaps these countries will give us some indication of the possible outcomes. In contrast, Africa and the Middle East countries are still exhibiting strong growth. I personally think this trend towards overall slower population growth is accelerating and the global population may peak earlier than projected but that is just my speculation.

POPULATION CHALLENGES

The native populations of the USA and Europe are breeding below their replacement rate. This trend is offset by significant legal and illegal immigration. There is very little discussion about the need to have an overall population policy. There are choices that need to be made by all countries. Most politicians and business leaders do not even want to consider the possibility of a declining population. In the long run they will have to. Contrastingly the population of the Middle East and Africa will continue to grow rapidly for the next 50 years due to their much higher birth rates.

It is difficult to know what overall immigration/emigration will be over the next 25 years. However, the Middle East and Africa are expected to more than double in size while the USA and Europe are either flat or grow modestly. The pressures on Europe and the USA will be unrelenting to allow more economic immigrants. Now we have many politicians and intellectuals that believe in open borders. If we have open borders, I estimate that in the next 40 years somewhere between 100 million and 200 million African and Middle East persons will come to Europe and the USA. Political resistance to more immigration, and particularly Muslim immigration, already exists in Europe. Additional accelerating immigration in Europe will lead to a political crisis. In the USA there is no meaningful discussion on what the appropriate immigration level should be. Today the discussion is about controlling illegal immigration. Not about what is the acceptable overall population growth. Most illegal immigrants are coming for economic reasons which is not a justification for asylum. The problem is that currently, under Biden, they are allowed in pending an asylum hearing in front of a judge. Unfortunately, these hearings are scheduled years in the future and most asylees never show up for their hearing. This problem did not exist under President Trump because he required the asylee to wait in Mexico until a judge adjudicated his or her case. The USA needs to get this situation under control before it can move on and have a sensible discussion about a long-term immigration policy.

Europe has been trying to deal with their immigration challenges for forty years. In the case of Europe many more of their immigrants are conservative Muslims who do not assimilate well. Europe needs to confront these issues head on or suffer greatly as a result. This means fences on its Eastern borders, like Hungary has. It means border controls at the outer boundaries of the Union. It means that there must be more expedient ways to identify genuine asylum seekers from economic refugees and the quick deportation of the latter. It is interesting to note that the European countries, like Hungary, that tasted the Ottoman Empire in the past are among the most resistant to Muslim immigration today. They remember.

The USA is only waking up now to understand it has a significant Muslim population (about 5 million), centered in St. Paul Minnesota and Dearborn Michigan. The protests about the Gaza/Israeli conflict have highlighted this. The USA should study what has happened in Europe and take measures to protect itself.

When you compare the differences in population growth with the differences in wealth (Chapter 1.2) it becomes intuitively obvious that many persons from the poorer countries with growing populations will want to move to the rich countries that are breeding below their replacement rate. This is already happening, and it is already causing a variety of economic and cultural issues. How we manage this re-arrangement of the world populations in the next 50 years is of immense importance to the future of the world.

The rich countries that are breeding below their replacement rate have three choices which are:

1. Population Growth (PG): Allow enough immigration such that the population continues to grow.
   - more immigration assures that markets and businesses will continue to grow
   - more immigration means more sharia (conservative) Muslims
   - more houses, factories, infrastructure and crowding
   - less countryside
   - more pollution
   - society can continue to support an ageing population

2. Zero Growth (ZG: allow only enough immigration to maintain the current population.
   - reduces the size of new investments required for infrastructure
   - better balance of cities with countryside
   - we can better manage sharia Muslim cultural conflicts
   - should be able to support ageing population with modest reforms
   - consumer business growth will flatten

3. Population Declines (PD)...manage declining population.
   - challenges to financially supporting aging population
   - with AI, new technology and access to global markets some growth may be possible but consumer demand will be less
   - reduce city sprawl, reduce pollution and increase natural countryside
   - focus on creating a more wholesome integrated society

Now there are 195 countries in the world. The 2023 current growth/shrinkage status is as follows:

Population Growth (PG).... greater than 0.5% growth   152 countries

In this group are practically all the African and Middle East countries. Syria and South Sudan come out tops with 6.4% and 4.8% per year growth respectively. Of the 152 countries in this category 55 are from Africa, 13 from the Middle East and 17 from Central America and the Caribbean

Zero Growth (ZG)……..growth between +0.5% and -0.5% 71 countries

The biggies are China +0.18%, S. Korea +0.23%, Japan -0.41%, Russia -0.48%

Population Declines (PD)……..declines in population greater than -0.5%……15 countries Georgia, Serbia, Estonia, Greece, Lithuania and Ukraine are in this category.

A critical issue for those countries who are choosing to allow immigration to either grow or maintain their current population level is assimilation. The USA is naive about these challenges. The USA takes pride that it has successfully integrated many immigrants over the years.

However, it ignores that it took about 150 years to fully integrate the large surge in immigrants from around 1870 to 1910 who were all from Europe and either Christian (Protestant and Catholic) or Jewish. The Europeans are currently confronting the fact that conservative (sharia law) Muslims do not assimilate in their Judeo-Christian culture. Conservative Muslims raised under sharia law are taught not to associate with Jews or Christians as a minimum and even to kill them. We saw this behavior exhibited recently by Hamas on October 7th, 2023. The resistance to assimilation by conservative Muslims is reinforced by the explicit strategy of "jihad by immigration". Jihad by immigration speaks to the view that the "struggle" for advancing Islam everywhere can be advanced by emigrating to a non-Muslim nation and over time making it majority Muslim because of the much higher birth rate of the Muslims. This is happening in Europe.

The takeaway is that if you are going to accept immigration make sure you control it ie. only legal immigrants and make sure their religion allows them to embrace and engage with the Judeo-Christian culture they are entering. Stated bluntly do not accept any sharia law Muslims. Having said that there are Muslims who are liberal and can assimilate. How to distinguish between very conservative and liberal Muslims without face-to-face interviews is difficult.

Americans have to accept that discriminating against persons because of their religion is acceptable. This is difficult for many Americans to do because of its perceived conflict with the first amendment of the US constitution which guarantees freedom of religion. The nation who has lived with this issue is Israel. Israel since 1948 has been surrounded by Muslims many of whom have wanted to and have tried to kill them. Israel has fought ten wars since 1948 with its Arab neighbors. During this time the situation has evolved. Today Israel is at peace with some of its neighboring Arab countries and 21% of the population of Israel is Arab and Muslim. There are even a small number of Muslims in the Israeli parliament and a few in the Israel Defense Force. If the USA decides to continue to allow legal Muslim immigration they should consult with Israel as to how best to do it.

The other issue with Muslims living in the US or Europe is their family life. Women and particularly daughters' behavior is strictly controlled by their male relatives. Islam is a religion created by a man for men. Women are subjugated by their husband and can easily be divorced. Daughters are discouraged from dating western men. Such activities dishonor the family and can be punished by beatings or even death at the hands of their father and brothers. Such honor killings occur in the USA and Europe every year. (see Chapter 2.2 for more detail)

Putting aside the issue of immigration there are lots of challenges for countries who choose ZG or PD. All nations need to have a debate on whether they want PG, ZG or PD. These are choices with immense social consequences. Nations should not drift into one reality or another. They should make a choice. Here, briefly, are some considerations:

Nations who consider other cultures inferior or more positively stated have a history and culture that is ritualized, different and deeply embedded do not welcome immigrants. Examples of such nations are China, South

Korea, N. Korea, Japan. These nations are either already in the PD mode or soon will be.

Capitalistic nations are kind of like Oliver Twist "Please sir can I have more." Free market capitalism is about growth. Growth by creating new technology driven markets but also just natural market size growth due to an expanding population. The USA is the best example of such a nation. The USA since the second world war has been on a growth binge creating tremendous wealth. Right now, there is a debate in the USA about the work versus personal time choices, but it is fairly new and the growth beast will be hard to control and that includes allowing lots of immigration, legal and illegal, into the USA. So again, the USA is strongly in the PG mode with lots of immigration and without any real debate at the government policy level about managing population growth.

What about ZG? There are not many examples. New Zealand just decided to reduce immigration because it was putting pressure on housing prices perhaps this is the beginning of a ZG policy for NZ. There are other countries that are ZG, not by choice, but by circumstance. these are countries that sit on the periphery of larger economic communities and attract modest immigration that makes up for their below replacement breeding rate and the emigration of some of their young people. Here are some examples:

Scotland population in 1960 5.1 million in 2020 5.4 million
Finland population about 5 million with recent annual growth about 0.1%
Denmark population in 1960 4.6 million in 2020 5.9 million
Portugal population in 1960 8.9 million in 2020 10.4 million
Italy population essentially flat at 59 million since 1980

source World Bank

These are all countries that are on the edge of large economic blocks. The dynamic is that some of their young people leave seeking better economic opportunities but with enough retirees, remote workers and very limited immigration the population growth has been very modest over 60 years.

In the very long run the world will have a population decline based on current trends. I think that after some decline it will stabilize. I think that human beings at some point faced with a shortage of labor for everyday tasks and an under occupancy of the existing infrastructure will start to have more children and the population will overall level out into a ZG result. This, however, is a speculation on my part and none of us can predict where this grand global experiment ends up.

CHAPTER 1.2

WEALTH DIFFERENCES

If population differences are the first drivers of emigration/immigration then the second, reinforcing, driver is wealth differences. The twentieth century was one of experiments. The world experimented with communism, fascism, socialism, theocracies, dictatorships, kingdoms, various forms of democracy, and a few things in between. During the twentieth century we had two world wars, multiple genocides, and numerous other conflicts. In the last sixty years there have been a number of significant events that have shaped today's global landscape. These are as follows:

1. The discrediting of Soviet-styled communism, leading to the replacement of the Union of Soviet Socialist Republics with the Russian Federation (1991)
2. The rapid expansion of global trade driven by the work of the World Trade Organization (WTO) and the creation of common markets such as the European Union (1993) and the North American Free Trade Association (NAFTA, 1994)
3. The emergence in the Middle East of initiatives to export terrorism with the intent to expand the presence of Islam and seek the destruction of Israel (Saudi Arabia, 1932; Iran, 1979; al- Qaeda, 1989; ISIS, 2011; Hamas 1987)
4. The decision by the Chinese Communist Party to transition the Chinese economy from an agrarian base to a more modern industrial basis while retaining tight totalitarian control.
5. The changes in Africa and many places in the Middle East following the withdrawal of the colonial powers from 1950 to 1975.

These changes have had an immense and ongoing impact on the world. If you are younger than thirty-five years in age, you may not realize that the current global situation is very new and continues to be fluid. Out of all these various initiatives the system that clearly delivers the best overall economic results is democracy allied with free market capitalism. Europe, the United States, Canada, New Zealand, Australia, Taiwan, Singapore, South Korea, Japan, Israel, Brazil, Chile to name a few have all prospered because democracy has enabled free market capitalism to deliver extraordinary increases in wealth. Although all of these named countries participated in this virtuous combination of democracy and free market capitalism, some did better than the rest. The leader is the United States, with the European countries and Japan not far behind. As you can see in figure 1, the trend for GDP per capita is strongly up and expected to continue to increase. That is the good news. The bad news is that we still have some politicians in the USA who still believe in "socialism". Examples of this are Bernie Sanders, AOC and on an erratic basis President Biden.

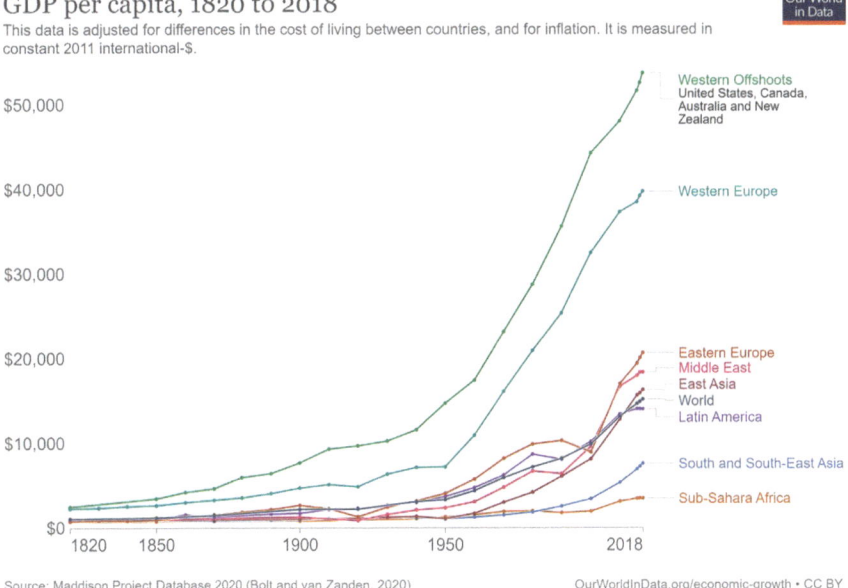

figure 1 WEALTH DIFFERENCES GDP PER CAPITA FOR SELECTED COUNTRIES

Unfortunately, many parts of the world have not participated in this democratic/free market growth. Africa and the Middle East are the areas that are struggling the most. If you exclude the countries in Africa and the Middle East that are lucky enough to have significant commodities (oil+) to export, then the GDP per capita for both regions shows little growth. Asia is enjoying wealth growth, pulled along by Japan, South Korea, China, India, and Taiwan. Looking forward, one can predict that these gaps between the richest regions of the world and the poorest will continue to widen. These differences created fewer problems sixty years ago. Today people living in Africa and the Middle East can, with the help of the internet, see and understand the much higher standard of living that others enjoy. It becomes a short step to say, "It looks so much better over there. I think I will go there." Europe is only a short boat ride, or a long walk or a short flight, from Africa and the Middle East. This is the "all aboard the European lifeboat" reality. The same thing is happening in the United States. Refugees can fly to Mexico City, rent a car, drive to the border, and present themselves to border control. Although the journey to the US is longer it can be cheaper and safer than paying smugglers to transport you from Turkey or Libya to Europe.

The opening, by Biden, of the United States southern borders has allowed for a consistent surge of illegal immigrants into the United States.

Why is global wealth expanding so fast? The reasons are different for the advanced economies compared to the developing ones. In the advanced economies, new innovative technology combined with a supply of entrepreneurs funded by venture capitalists is the main fuel for this continuing wealth growth. In the developing economies, the basic driver is the transition from an agrarian economy to an industrial economy. When millions of subsistence level farmers become factory workers, the increases in global productivity drive immense wealth increases. However, this transformation is not happening equally everywhere in the world. For it to happen, there has to be a functioning government with relatively non-corrupt institutions in place.

When you look around the world today, you see billions of people who are ready to make the same journey from being a farmer to doing something of much greater value. The world GDP is going to continue to grow rapidly but wealth disparities will continue. The World Bank projects that world GDP will increase significantly in the next twenty years. Some folks think that because the income levels in developed countries are getting high, we should reduce production and consumption and commit to a different lifestyle, one with more leisure and community- oriented activities. I think that these people are missing the fact that China would not have been able to pull itself out of poverty without the consumer demand from Europe and North America. The best form of foreign aid is to buy products or raw materials that are made possible by cheap labor in poor countries. Such policies increase the chances that people will stay where they are rather than trying to emigrate.

As you consider all the regions of the world, Africa stands out as the least capable to create viable futures for its citizens. Because of political correctness, the world cannot recognize Africa as a failed continent. We are afraid to say it.

CHAPTER 1.3

IMMIGRATION- IT IS "EASY"

Actually, the title to this chapter is wrong. It should be "Legal immigration is hard-Illegal immigration is easy". N. America and Europe are extremely wealthy. Most of Africa, the Middle East and Central America are poor. These poor people see Europe and the USA as an immense opportunity if they can get there and stay. Let me count the ways that this is possible:

Legal Immigration.

Takes 1-4 years, moderately expensive and no guarantee of success.

Illegal Immigration

Get accepted by a college, get a student visa and just stay.
Get a tourist visa, fly in and just stay.
Slip across the border undetected and just stay.
Present yourself at the border and claim asylum.

If you are in the country illegally the first thing you need to do is figure out how to get work. If you are at the bottom of the food chain you can get hired for cash. If you want a regular job at a business you need credentials. You need a driving license and a social security number. You either try to get forged documents or assume the identity of a dead person and work from there.

If you are an asylee you will have been issued a Form I-94 at entry which gets you a employment authorization document (EAD). With these documents you can get a social security card. You are cleared to work until your court date which is years down the road at which time you either need a very good story or you just fade away.

The bottom line is that the governments in the US and Europe have no idea as to how many illegal immigrants they have in their countries. They have actually given up guessing. In the USA they are not very interested in finding and deporting illegal immigrants. I once had responsibility for a metal cabinet plant in Burbank CA. It had about 450 employees mostly Hispanic. One day in the 1990's the immigration people came in and did a sweep. They found about 80 employees who were illegals. We had to let them go with no consequence to them and hire new ones. We asked the immigration folks if we could run these new employees through their system to make sure they were legal. They declined to cooperate. By the way all these "80 illegals" had social security cards that the system nominally processed.

The government's estimate for the number of illegal immigrants is about 10 million. This number is derived from the number of people who self report on the US census survey as foreign born. It is a calculation that uses the number of people who self-report as foreign born, subtracts the known foreign born resident number, and then adds 10%. It is a laughable estimate. The problem is that if you are living illegally in the United States, it seems highly unlikely that you will document your presence on a government census form. The federal government in testimony before Congress admits that it just does not know how many persons overstay visas to be in the United States.

Yale School of management estimated in 2018, using a variety of other metrics such as building permits, foreign money remittances, and schoolchildren's attendance records, that the number of illegals in the United States was in the range of 16 to 29 million.

In 2022 the Government reported that there were 850,000 visa "overstays". It was 702000 in 2017. It was 680000 in2020. We seem to be running about 750000 overstays a year. Since we have no precise way of recording exits no one seems to know how many of these overstays have never left.

Since 2020 the Border Patrol has processed 8.5 million illegals. Guesses for "gotaways" are 1.5 to 2 million since 2020. That is a total of about 10 million since Biden took office.

Taking all these numbers we could easily have as many as 30 million illegals in the country. The US government is clearly not interested in admitting that they have lost control of our borders and have no idea how many illegal immigrants are in the country.

We have an E-Verify program which is meant to prevent illegals from gaining employment. It is not mandatory and it is only used in certain states for government contracts. A number of years ago the government launched a program to record when persons who had entered the country on a visa left the country. It was voluntary when launched. I actually used it a couple of times. It quickly disappeared. Part of the reason that the government does not want to know is the issue of granting amnesty which is tied to immigration reform. The foundation of current immigration law was passed in 1976. Although there have been a number of tweaks to this law the 1976 law provides the foundation of immigration today. The 1976 law places a priority on admitting persons with family connections in the USA. Europe also places a priority on family reunification. These laws are not what we need today.

The difficult issue is amnesty. The last time amnesty was granted to illegals was 1986 when Reagan was President. So today we have the accumulation of 38 years of illegal immigrants but still the US government's estimate is the number is flat at about 11 million. We have the DACA folks who are children who were brought into the USA by illegal entry parents. There are 545 thousand DACA persons which only accounts for those who entered prior to 2007. What should happen with these DACA persons has been under debate for some time. A more interesting issue is that If you are born in the USA you are entitled to US citizenship. This means that if you want to gold plate your illegal status have a baby in the USA and it is almost guaranteed that you will never be deported. Dealing with amnesty is the biggest problem in addressing immigration reform. The politicians in Washington DC are afraid to admit to the voters their negligence in minding our borders. As I write Biden is making it worse day by day. Trump when in office shut down the southern border by requiring asylum seekers to stay in Mexico until their asylum claim was adjudicated.

THOUGHTS ON WHAT IS A SMART IMMIGRATION POLICY

Smart immigration is the right number of workers with the right skill set who will assimilate easily:

Ideally a nation would decide ever year how many immigrants they need in the following say 36 months.

They would have criteria such as work experience, education and being able to speak their host's country language.

They would avoid persons whose value systems and culture increased the risk of non- assimilation.

Two countries that do the "immigration thing " in a smart way are Canada and Australia.

Here are Canada's criteria:

- a passport or travel document.
- language test results.
- proof of Canadian education or an educational credential assessment report for immigration purposes if.
- provincial nomination (if you have one).
- written job offer from an employer in Canada (if you have one).
- proof of work experience.
- certificate of qualification in a trade occupation issued by a Canadian province or territory (if you have one).
- proof of funds.

If you want to go to the head of the queue get a job offer from a Canadian employer. Australia's criteria are similar but a little more complicated.

Here are France's criteria:

French Residency Permit Requirements

- Completed application form.
- Valid passport.
- Proof of purpose such as an employment contract or study invitation.
- Proof of funds such as a bank statement.
- Evidence of accommodation such as a rental agreement or purchase contract.
- Health insurance.

In contrast the US immigration rules place a heavy emphasis on family connections.

Clearly practically all unscreened illegal immigrants in to the USA do not meet these criteria. Biden's policies have allowed in 10 million unscreened persons in the last three years causing social and economic harm on a large scale. Part of the problem is that the USA is very wealthy and some of our politicians have "bleeding hearts" or more cynically they believe that in the long run these new immigrants will translate into more votes and power for their party. However, the price is paid by our working citizens who have to compete with these new guests. Wages are restricted and health care costs rise and the national debt continues to grow. Biden's policies are simply bad, bad, bad.

The choices required to be smart on immigration are hard and involve conflict which many Christians struggle with. Here is a story that forces you to examine the choice:

THE LIFEBOAT DILEMMA based on events in the Mediterranean

You and your wife and two children are sailing in the Mediterranean in a 30ft. boat. Suddenly you see people in the water not too far away. Lots of people maybe 200 or so. You sail closer. As you get close to the nearest persons they cry out for help. You start to pull aboard a few people but soon your wife says to you we cannot save all these people. If we are not careful they will swamp the boat and then we will all be in the water. As you see more and more people swimming towards your boat you realize your wife is right. You start your engines and start to back away. At this point you have rescued 6 people. No sooner than you start to back away when a lady who speaks good English says "you must try and save my sister". She is a Christian. I am a Christian. These other people are Muslims. Before our boat sank, when it was in trouble, they threw all the Christians overboard. They tried to kill us. My sister is just over there. This man in your boat is one of the Muslims who threw us overboard. You are a good Christian man please save my sister and throw this man back into the water. Such are the dilemmas in dealing with immigration.

TAKEAWAY. You have to choose and in the act of choosing you choose the greater good and in doing so you discriminate.

CHAPTER 2.1

FOR GOD'S SAKE

Global Religions

Worldwide, more than eight in ten people identify with a religious group. The makeup by religion is shown in the following table.

Size and Projected Growth of Major Religious Groups

	2010 POPULATION	% OF WORLD POPULATION IN 2010	PROJECTED 2050 POPULATION	% OF WORLD POPULATION IN 2050	POPULATION GROWTH 2010-2050
Christians	2,168,330,000	31.4%	2,918,070,000	31.4%	749,740,000
Muslims	1,599,700,000	23.2	2,761,480,000	29.7	1,161,780,000
Unaffiliated	1,131,150,000	16.4	1,230,340,000	13.2	99,190,000
Hindus	1,032,210,000	15.0	1,384,360,000	14.9	352,140,000
Buddhists	487,760,000	7.1	486,270,000	5.2	-1,490,000
Folk Religions	404,690,000	5.9	449,140,000	4.8	44,450,000
Other Religions	58,150,000	0.8	61,450,000	0.7	3,300,000
Jews	13,860,000	0.2	16,090,000	0.2	2,230,000
World total	6,895,850,000	100.0	9,307,190,000	100.0	2,411,340,000

Source: The Future of World Religions: Population Growth Projections, 2010-2050
PEW RESEARCH CENTER

The Christians are fairly evenly distributed around the world. In contrast, the Muslims occupy an arc that has an east–west axis from Indonesia to Morocco and a south north axis from the immediate sub-Sahara countries up to Albania and Uzbekistan. These regions of Muslim influence tend to mirror the reach of the Persian Empire which was founded around 550 BCE and went in to decline after 330 BCE. The percentage of all Christians and Muslims who live in each geographic region is as follows:

TABLE Percent by Geographic Region of Christianity and Islam

	Europe	N. America	S. America	Africa	Asia (includes Middle East)
Christians	24	23	21	21	12
Muslims	3	0.4	0.1	29	69

Interestingly, as noted above, it is expected that by 2050 the following will be true:

The number of Muslims will nearly equal the number of Christians around the world. Atheists, agnostics, and other people who do not affiliate with any religion though increasing in countries such as the United States and France will make up a declining share of the world's total population.

The global Buddhist population will be about the same size it was in 2010, whereas the Hindu and Jewish populations will be larger than they are today.

In Europe, Muslims will make up 10 percent of the overall population, up from 5 percent in 2022 due to their higher birth rates.

India will retain a Hindu majority but also will have one of the largest Muslim populations of any country in the world, just behind Indonesia and similar to Pakistan.

In the United States, Christians, which made up more than three-quarters of the population in 2010, will account for two-thirds of the population in 2050, and Judaism will be replaced by Islam as the largest non-Christian religion.

Four out of every ten Christians in the world will live in sub-Saharan Africa.

As a gross generalization you can divide the world religions in to four buckets: the Jews, the Christians, the Muslims, the Hindu and all the rest. The history of the Muslims is that they are not good neighbors or good guests. The Buddhists in Myanmar certainly have bad relations with the Muslim Rohingya minority in their country. India is barely on speaking terms with its Muslim neighbor, Pakistan. Russia struggles to coexist with the Muslim communities within its own boundaries, like in Chechnya, and with its Muslim neighbors. Azerbaijan and Armenia have continuing hostilities. Similarly, in Africa there is friction between the Muslim sub-Saharan countries and their Christian neighbors to the south. The fighting in the Central African Republic between Muslim militia and Christian militia is typical. The island of Cyprus is an independent republic divided into Greek (Christian) and Turkish (Muslim) zones. The Chinese government has an ongoing suppression of the Uyghur Muslim people, trying to limit their ability to practice and proselytize their religion. In Thailand the Mara Patani Muslim organization continues its insurgency in the south. Now in all these cases it is difficult to determine who bears most of the blame for the situation. However, the pattern is that Muslims do not play well with their neighbors. The all-encompassing philosophy of Islam, coupled with Muslim intolerance for those of other faiths, is the root cause of the friction. Muslims have been on an intolerant expansionist mission for the last fourteen hundred years since their start in 610AD. In Europe and North America we do not teach this history, but Christendom and Islam are old enemies.

You would think that Judaism, Christianity, and Islam should get along famously because they share so much common history. The opposite is true. The main common aspect is that they worship the same God, and the main difference is about who is the true prophet. The Muslims believe that Muhammad is the true and last prophet and that the Koran was directly revealed to him by God via the Archangel Gabriel. The Koran includes recognition of some of the prophets and messengers or apostles who also represent the Jewish and Christian religions. Amid the about twenty-eight main prophets and messengers recognized in the Koran are included Adam (the first prophet on earth), Noah, Abraham, Moses, and Jesus. In trying to understand the conflicts between these religions, it is important to distinguish between what their adherents do versus what is written. Every religion has lots of writings. The important thing is to follow the behavior of the adherents, not the religion's written word.

It is important to discuss the Jews because, although there are only sixteen million of them, they have played a significant role relative to the Christians and Muslims. The obvious question is, why are there so few Jews when they have existed and been breeding for over three thousand years? The answer is that many have been killed or were forcefully converted in large numbers over the last three thousand years. The Jews have suffered at the hands of the Assyrians (733 BC), the Babylonians (597 BC), the Romans, the Christians, and lastly the Muslims. Because of all these events, the Jews who were not killed or converted were scattered across Europe, North Africa, and the United States (the Diaspora). With the establishment of Israel in 1948, many of these Jews returned to their ancestral lands. Given this history, the Jews understandably just want to be left alone. Unfortunately, their presence on previously caliphate lands, especially Jerusalem, is viewed by some Muslims as unacceptable and thus the calls by Iran and others for their destruction.

The Christian religion obviously came after Judaism, and is today a "nice" religion. Christians are today accepting of all other religions. This was not always the case. In the past Christians fought many holy wars. Today Christians are like the Beatles and believe that "all you need is love." All the Christian religions have a corporate feel. There are hierarchal organizations that have formal policies. There is a consistency in the product offered.

The above discussion is the nuts and bolts of religion. Religion is much more. All of our nations, all of our cultures have a connection to religion. Religion is the foundation of any search of how to be a good human being. Unfortunately some religious believers take their beliefs too far. In the past individuals have been crucified, burnt at the stake and worse. Armies have fought each other in "holy wars". A place where people are still fighting over is Jerusalem. Jerusalem is a special place in Judaic, Christian and Muslim culture. Jerusalem is the location that Moses was trying to reach…..the "Promised Land". Jesus was born close to Jerusalem in Bethlehem, lived his life in the vicinity and was crucified and rose again there. Jerusalem is where Allah made his "night journey" to. Today Jerusalem is the third holiest site in Islam.

Prior to Jesus being born Jerusalem was fought over by the Romans, the Persians and the Greeks. In the last two thousand years it has been fought over by the Muslims and Christians. Many crusades in the 1100 to 1300 period were directed at Jerusalem. The venom that Iran has with Israel has a great deal to do with who should control Jerusalem added to the historical enmity of Muslims to Jews. It is all very sad but still very real.

CHAPTER 2.2

ISLAM

The Judaism and Islam religion communities are very similar. In making this comparison I am comparing the most conservative versions of both faiths.

- They both worship the same God.
- Women are subjugated to men.
- Women and men worship separately in their Temple or Mosque.
- They both do not eat pork.
- The primary focus of their life is their religion.

The differences are:

The Jews believe Moses had a relationship with God and his teachings came from GOD through him. Moses lived around 1500BC and he lead the Hebrews out of Egypt first to the Sinai and later to Mt. Nebo in Trans Jordan where he died in sight of the "Promised Land".

The Muslims believe that Muhammad received his teachings from the Archangel Gabriel in 610AD in a cave near Mecca, in the Arabian Peninsula. He started preaching in Mecca but later moved to Medina where he raised an army to promote his teachings. Islam recognizes all the previous Jewish and Christian prophets as part of their shared history.

Since Islam established itself in the Arabian Peninsula there has been continued conflict between the Jewish, Christian and Muslim faiths. The Christian crusades are part of that conflict. The Christian crusades were many and continued for 200 years (1095-1291). During that time Jerusalem was occupied and managed by Christians for 88 years. Since about 1200 Jerusalem has been occupied by Muslims. Starting in 1948 the Jews have controlled Jerusalem. These struggles between the three religions have been going on for over two thousand years.

Simply stated the current status of the three religions is that:

The Jews just want to be left alone but as long as they control Jerusalem and the surrounding territory they will be subject to attack by Muslims.

The Christians think that "all we need is love".

The Muslims want to dominate the Middle East and in particular control Jerusalem. Additionaly there is a Muslim rivalry between the Ottomans (Turkey), the Shias (Iran) and the Sunnis (Saudi Arabia).

The major conflict today is with conservative Muslims living in Europe and the USA. They do not want to abandon their traditional way of life but at the same time they want the economic benefits of living in the West. The conflict between conservative Muslims and their hosts in the USA and Europe is unavoidable. The practical areas of conflict come from the differences in family life. Here are some everyday conflicts:

Some Muslims are offended by non-Muslims defiling Muhammed. An example of this is displaying a photograph/drawing showing the image of Muhammad. This has resulted in people being killed even though the behavior was innocent such as a teacher doing so in a classroom environment.

You have to accept that many of their women are under the control of the men. Women in many Muslim countries are second class citizens. Daughters will often be married according to the wishes of her male relatives. Women are disadvantage in divorce and inheritance matters.

You will have to accept that some Muslims instead of fitting into the western way of life will campaign for exceptions based on their religion. Examples would be dress, religious holidays and no exposure to alcohol even when it is part of their job duties. Female face coverings have been an issue in Europe where identity is required for voting. Airport security is another potential problem. Muslim family courts exist in the UK to help process Muslim family disputes.

You will have to accept that certain girls will, at the age of about 10, be taken back to their home countries to have their clitoris cut out and probably also their labia (the vaginal lips). This is the process of Female Genital Mutilation (FGM). 125 million Muslim women have been mutilated (WHO). With 2 billion Muslims worldwide, 50% female, 125 million is approximately 12.5% of all Muslim women.

You will have to accept that there will be occasional honor killings. These typically happen when a young Muslim girl dishonors her family by engaging with non-Muslim boys. An honor killing is carried out by a father sometimes with the help of brothers. These are rare. But they do great damage by sending a signal to other young Muslim women "Do not socialize at all with non-Muslim boys". It is estimated that there are 5000 honor killings each year and yes they do occur in the USA (27 per year) and Europe (no good data). It is generally agreed that the actual number of honor killings is higher than reported because many deaths are either not reported or reported but not as honor killings.

You will have to live with Muslim men grooming and then raping young vulnerable non-Muslim girls as happened in Rotherham in the UK with 1400 children being abused between 1997 and 2013. This occurs because these girls are non-Muslim, dress in immodest ways and depending how you want to evaluate the situation there is some justification in the Koran for making sex slaves out of "conquered" non-Muslim women. This happened in recent time when ISIS was active in Syria. It also happens with some frequency throughout Europe.

Now these are difficult things to ignore and they are only perpetrated by a minority. The evidence is we do tend to ignore them or downplay them. We ignore them because we support religious tolerance even when there are acts that are in conflict with our culture and our laws. We are afraid that any straightforward discussion will be categorized as bigotry. It is important to note that such practices are restricted to a minority of Muslims. However, it is also fair to say that the law-abiding Muslim communities under the leadership of their Imams are reluctant to aggressively work with the police to root out such behavior. You could argue that similar criminal behavior already exists in the US and Europe. However, that is something we have to live with. The question in front of us is whether we want to invite more criminal activity into our communities. It is not a question of discrimination for the US or the UK to question whether or not they want more Muslim immigration. It is a justifiable public debate on what is the immigration policy that best serves the needs of the country. The issue is whether genuine assimilation of conservative Muslims can happen. These cultural issues will take time, a lot of time, to disappear.

CHAPTER 3.1

HOW THE USA GOT RICH

The Wealth Status

How are we doing in the West? "Really well" is the answer if we are just talking about wealth. Considering economic wellbeing and individual human rights, democracy has delivered the best overall results. Europe, the United States, Canada, New Zealand, Australia, Taiwan, Singapore, South Korea, Japan, Israel, Brazil, and Chile have all prospered, but not just because of democracy. They have prospered because democratic institutions enable free market capitalism to deliver extraordinary increases in wealth. Although all of these named countries participated in this virtuous combination of democracy and free market capitalism, some did better than the rest. The leader is the United States, with the European countries and Japan not far behind. As you can see, the trend for GDP per capita is strongly up and expected to continue to increase. That is the good news.

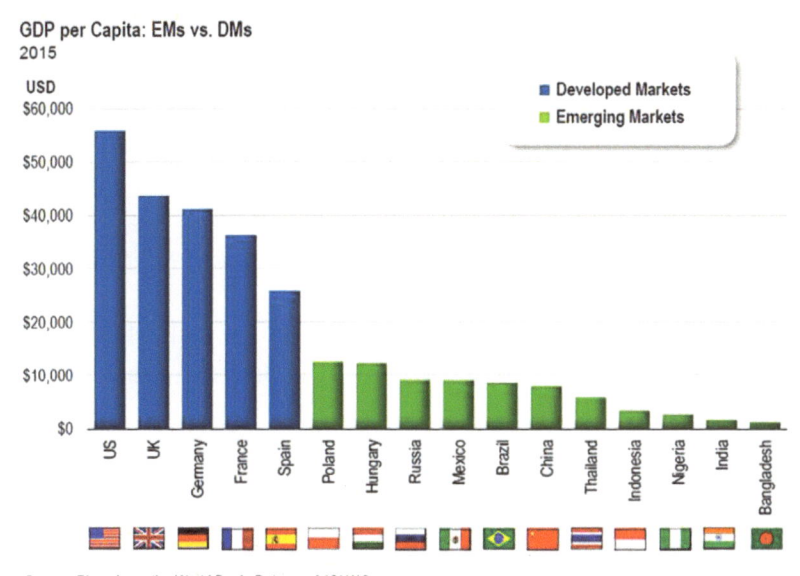

GDP per Capita: EMs vs. DMs
2015

Source: Bloomberg, the World Bank. Data as of 10/4/16.

— Continued

The Golden Goose: Democracy and Free Market Capitalism

The extraordinary wealth increases the West has enjoyed are the result of practicing free market capitalism. Free market capitalism performs at its best in certain environments. It requires certain governmental/institutional conditions to set the table, so to speak. In addition, it requires individuals who want to play the game. The people who want to play the game are the entrepreneurs, and they, in turn, need the investors who are willing to take the risk of investing in their business.

The role of government is to ensure the following things:

The individual ownership of property

The ability to receive patents on innovative ideas and technology Regulations that ensure free and competitive markets Regulations to enable financial markets to function

Tax policies that are supportive of wealth creation by individuals Investments that support fundamental research

A commitment to fair and equal treatment by the government (empirical evidence shows that this requires a separation of religion from the state)

An independent judiciary system to police the government and businesses A system to deal with business failure quickly

The enabling infrastructure, such as airports and roads

All of these requirements from government exist, not perfectly, but to the greatest extent in the United States, Europe, and certain other advanced economies. We take them for granted.

However, many countries do not have such an institutional structure.

Culture also plays a big role in supporting a successful free market economy. Important ingredients are as follows:

We need a supply of highly educated, hardworking individuals to lead these startup companies. We are fortunate in the US that we have a history of successful startup leaders such as Bill Gates (Microsoft), Steve Jobs (Apple), Mark Zuckerberg (Facebook), Jeff Bezos (Amazon), and Elon Musk (Tesla)… see footnote

The willingness of individuals to provide the funds for start-up companies through crowd investing, angel investing, and venture capital. Again, the United States is particularly strong in this area.

Access to technology and the engineers who understand it. Between the universities, the government's national laboratories, and privately funded work, the United States is well positioned.

The acceptance that many companies fail and the willingness to give individuals a second chance. Again, the United States accepts that failure is an unavoidable part of the creative destruction of capitalism and evolving technologies. The US bankruptcy laws allow for the rapid resolution of business failures and a redeployment of the assets.

There are many places in the world where free market capitalism has very little chance. Also, there is no place in the world where a 100 percent pure example of free market capitalism exists. Milton Friedman used to hold up Hong Kong as a great example of free market capitalism, but that was before the British left and it came under the wing of Beijing.

The US Success Formula

The United States is the most successful large entrepreneurial society in the world. There are successful smaller ones, like Singapore. Europe has tried to follow the United States' model, but it has had less success, mainly because of the cultural factors discussed above. While the US and European government setups are similar, the United States has a much more entrepreneurial tradition. In particular, the United States has a very embedded small business tradition. The desire of many US citizens to have their own business, to be their own boss, is strong.

Individuals start businesses to offer products and services to their fellow citizens, their customers. The customer chooses to buy the product or service that he or she considers to be the best deal. The business that offers the best deal grows and starts to make profits. The customer is happy, and the entrepreneur who worked hard to offer the best deal is rewarded.

In the United States people tend to know the names of some large corporations and think of business as being mainly large corporations. It turns out that small businesses (businesses with fewer than 500 employees) are equally important to the US economy. There are 33.2 million small businesses and only 20,868 companies with more than 500 employees. Following are some facts (1994-2020 data).

Small businesses, those with less than 500 employees, makeup:

- 99.9 percent of US employer firms
- 62.7 percent net of new private sector jobs
- 46.4 percent of private sector employment
- 49.4 percent of private sector payroll
- 46 percent of private sector output
- 43 percent of high-tech employment
- 97.3 percent of firms exporting goods
- 32.6 percent of exporting value

Some people resent the success of entrepreneurs who create small businesses. Let me tell you, it is not easy to start a business and every year many small businesses fail.

68% survive at least 2 years
49% survive 5 years
34% survive 10 years

Based on these data, you can see that it is not easy to be successful. About half of small businesses survive five years or more, and about one third survive ten years or more. So only a minority of small businesses are successful over the long term.

Small businesses, in any event, are extremely important to the US economy. They do the following things:

Provide the goods and services you need
Create the majority of new private sector jobs
Obviously pay a lot of taxes

In other words, small businesses are the engine of the economy. If you tax and regulate small businesses too much, as is done in Europe, then you get less: fewer new businesses, higher prices, fewer jobs, and less tax revenue. You get the idea.

In addition, the United States benefits from an array of large global companies. Building a successful global company, in most cases, takes decades. Once built, such companies should have sustaining competitive advantages if they are well managed. The innovation in the economy happens most often in small start-up companies. As these innovative companies are successful and grow, many of them are bought up by the larger companies. The United States has a powerful wealth-creation system based on its small businesses and its larger global corporations.

I believe that current cultures strongly reflect their religious history. Different religions vary in the constraints they place on the individual. The Asian philosophies and the Protestant Christian religions place the least constraints on the minds of individuals. Innovation and progress comes best from individuals accountable only to God or perhaps only to yourself if you are an atheist. This freedom of the minds of individuals to explore, to innovate, to invent, to lead speaks to the "power of one" resident in certain individuals. The table above says that all the Christian based countries plus Asia are suited to the wealth creation that comes with democracy plus free market capitalism. The creation of national wealth is not racially dependent, it is systems and culturally dependent. Who are the races that are rich and/or getting rich? They are Europeans, all of North and South America, Japanese, South Koreans (not North Koreans), Chinese, India and certain other Asian Nations. Economic success is not a result of race or ethnic origin. In the beginning it was chance. It was not about white supremacy. The Chinese, Indians and the Middle East were arguably more civilized at earlier times than Europe. However, they were not able to put together all the pieces of the "Golden Goose' formula outlined earlier. The scary thing about the success of Western Civilization is that many people have no idea of the Golden Goose formula. Most people take the economic prosperity they have for granted and assume it cannot be taken away. Europe has already drifted away from the formula. The USA is at risk of following Europe.

Socialists like Bernie Sanders and Kamala Harris personify this risk.

The matter of China is interesting in this regard, as China is not a democracy. China is a very technically competent authoritarian regime. China has not yet demonstrated that it can be a successful broad based entrepreneurial society. So far it has moved millions of peasant farmers into cities to work in factories and selectively "borrowed" technical knowhow from European and US companies. China's success is primarily based on selling products made from low cost labor to the United States and Europe. China cannot fully develop under its current totalitarian system. To fully develop, it will need a proper legal system, an independent judiciary, and human rights.

Muslim countries and Africa have fundamental barriers to creating wealth. At a minimum, all Muslim countries need to separate religion from the state and create proper legal systems (not sharia) if they are to have any chance of becoming successful capitalist economies. Obviously such suggestions are total nonstarters with Iran and Saudi Arabia. As I have previously discussed, strong group cultures inhibit the spirit of the individual, and most, if not all, innovation comes from individuals. If the Middle East did not have oil as a major source of revenue it would be a sad place. Africa and the Muslim countries also have the additional challenge of very high birth rates, which dilutes the effect of any GDP growth.

However, it is not impossible for a Muslim country to have a successful capitalist economy. Turkey in 1923 created a constitution that separated mosque from state, created a separate judiciary and developed other attributes of a modern state. In the intervening years, Turkey has increased its nominal GDP per capita from very little to $10,500. Tunisia is another Muslim country that is trying to go in the right direction. These Muslim countries are the exceptions. Most others are not democratic, and, if they are not theocracies, Islam is a fundamental part of their government and judiciary. You might ask about the rich Muslim countries, the ones that have oil and gas to sell.

These countries are squandering the opportunity to implement changes in their economy and in their social structure before their oil money runs out. The core dilemma for a Muslim is that if the primary purpose of life is to worship and obey the Prophet Muhammad, then it is difficult to give a higher priority to any other human activity. Also by not involving women in productive economic activity, these Muslim countries are limiting their productive capacity. Last, sharia law is not capitalism friendly. The example in the Middle East that stands in contrast to the Muslim nations is Israel. Israel started with very little in 1948. Today its GDP per capita is $35,702. This is a country where 21 percent of the population is Arab with no intrinsic advantages. Israel has no official state religion. Why has Israel done so well when its Arab neighbors have not? The answer is that Israel meets the criteria above for an appropriate government structure combined with a free market capitalistic culture. That plus seventy six years of hard work is why Israel is where it is today.

Technology, a Necessary Ingredient in Wealth Creation

I would be remiss if, in discussing wealth creation, I did not dwell on the vital importance of technology. As an engineer who during my career had responsibility for the development of a variety of products such as nuclear reactors, distribution transformers, medical diagnostic devices, industrial tools and automotive devices, I understand that it is the new and better mousetrap that opens doors and creates business success. The United States has the most comprehensive technology base in the world. The global software and hardware businesses were all created from US technical innovations. There are many other examples. After the United

States comes Europe and Japan. Then there is a significant gap between these three and whoever is number four.

Footnote on business leaders: Increasingly the CEO and CFO leaders of many of our successful companies are Asian. Here are some examples:

Nardelli.	CEO Microsoft
Pichai.	CEO Google & Alphabet
Huang.	CEO Nividia
Su.	CEO Advanced Micro Devices
ZS.	CEO Chaudry
Narayen.	CEO Adobe
Tan.	CEO Broadcom
Yuan.	CEO Zoom
Nooyi.	CEO PepsiCo
Mehrota.	CEO Micron
Krishna.	CEO IBM
Narasimhan	CEO StarBucks

There are a total of 42 Asian CEO's in the Fortune 500. There is also many CFO's that are Asian. These Asians have risen to their positions because they are highly educated and from childhood they grew up in homes where education and hard work were prescribed. We are fortunate to have them. They reflect the meriotratic nature of US business.

CHAPTER 3.2

HOW THE MIDDLE EAST GOT RICH….hint OIL

The answer is of course oil. Oil was first discovered in Iran in 1908, in Iraq in 1927, in Bahrain in 1931, and in Saudi Arabia in 1938. By the time the Second World War was over, the automobile was coming of age and the demand for oil was rising rapidly. This combination promised immense riches to the countries with oil, such as Iran, Iraq, and Saudi Arabia. Soon oil became the main source of revenue for the oil producing countries. It allowed the ruling families to buy loyalty as opposed to earning it. It reduced the need for political reform and also reduced the need to develop an alternate economy to oil. In that sense, oil is a curse to the Middle East.

For many countries it has hidden the failure of their society to respond to the needs of their populace and to engage with the global community.

The relationship of the West and the Middle East is long and complex. How the oil fields were developed is a key part of that history. Western companies were very involved in the discovery of oil and its development. This partnership has been both beneficial but also damaging at times to the relationships of Iran and Saudi Arabia with the USA.

The British company that discovered oil in Iran made a deal to keep 84 percent of the profits for sixty years. As the oil profits exploded, this led to an ongoing and neverending disagreement between the British and the Persians. These disagreements finally came to a head when in 1951, following the assassination of the previous prime minister, the new prime minister, Mohammed Mossadegh, nationalized the oil industry. This led to an embargo by the British, which in turn led to the Central Intelligence Agency getting involved and conspiring with the Shah so that in 1952 Mossadegh was arrested, a new deal was put in place, and the oil began to flow again. The new deal was a fifty-fifty deal that included US oil companies. During all of this, the pro-Western Shah lost significant credibility with his people. This history created part of the resentment that triggered the 1979 Iranian Revolution and the ouster of the Shah. This history is part of the reason why certain Iranians resent the West. For seventy years, British and US oil companies backed by their governments overplayed their hand and exploited Iran.

The deal concerning oil in Saudi Arabia was similar to Iran's, with a US oil company being the beneficiary. By 1950 the Saudis, after threatening nationalization, achieved a fifty-fifty split, and in 1980 they achieved total control over their oil resources. Again, it is easy to appreciate that Saudis might resent the West, and in particular the United States. However, the Saudis must put any resentment in their back pocket because they need the United States and the United Kingdom to supply them with armaments. Iran has Russia to supply it armaments.

Europe Leaves; Israel Is Founded

After the Second World War the Middle East after having been part of the Ottoman Empire until 1920 and then ruled over by the French and British since 1920 was set free. The British and French protectorate roles had been established as part of the partitioning of the Ottoman Empire following the First World War. Britain had oversight of Egypt, Palestine, Transjordan, Kuwait, Bahrein, Qatar and part of Syria. France had oversight of Lebanon, part of Syria and Iraq. The departure of the British and French involved, in some cases, establishing the boundaries of new countries with new rulers. There had been discussions of creating within Palestine a home for the Jewish people dating back to the Balfour Declaration of 1917. The intent to do this was embraced by the League of Nations and incorporated in the mandate to the British in 1922. In 1947 the United Nations continued to work on how to best resolve the partition of Palestine between the Jews and the Arabs. The General Assembly approved a plan dividing Palestine and having Jerusalem operate under an independent trusteeship. The Jews accepted the plan. The Arabs rejected the plan. Prior to the British leaving in May of 1948 there was significant fighting between the Jews and the Arabs. At this time, although there was a proposed plan for partition, there was no agreement.

On the day that the British mandate ended (May 14, 1948), David Ben-Gurion announced the creation of the state of Israel. On the following day, the United States recognized Israel. On the same day, Arab forces from Egypt, Transjordan, Syria, Iraq, and Lebanon invaded Palestine, with the intent to occupy certain areas. Troops from Saudi Arabia and Yemen also participated. Ten months later, Israel won the war and expanded its territorial control. Since 1948, the Arab nations have fought a total of ten wars with Israel, with little success. Clearly the creation of the state of Israel was a willful act by the Jewish people. It is also clear that the various Arab nations that opposed it had a variety of individual and selfish motivations. The situation remains as an open wound, with Israel's control over Jerusalem being an especially contentious issue.

The Theocracies

In the very early days of Islam, Muslims used to pray facing Jerusalem. Later they changed this to Mecca. Today Jerusalem is the third holiest city in Islam. Prior to the establishment of Israel, the religious leaders of Iran and the Arab nations petitioned strongly against the United Nations proposal. Over the last seventy years, the religious hierarchy of Iran has not wavered in their opposition to the presence of the Zionists in Jerusalem (Quds) and on the lands of Palestine.

They have funded Hamas in Gaza, Hezbollah in Lebanon and the Houthis in Yemen to fight and harass Israel. Iran considers the requirement to rid Palestine and Jerusalem of the Jews as a religious obligation and appears to be immovable in its pursuit of this goal. We should take the Iranians at their word. Over the last seventy years other nations have been more pragmatic. Back in 1948, Jordan and Egypt both participated in invading and trying to defeat Israel. Today Jordan and Egypt live at peace and cooperate with Israel. Saudi Arabia under the Abraham Agreements is now interested in building a relationship with Israel. Syria, as a Shia led country, has also consistently opposed Israel. Right now, Syria has its own problems. The dominating issue for Israel is the intransigence of Iran.

Muhammed and the Koran call for the elimination of the Jews, and Islam has successfully followed that path for the last thirteen hundred years. At the heart of the Islam of Iran and Saudi Arabia is a religious obligation to advance the reach of Islam and to do it in a way that requires others to convert, pay a tax, be enslaved, or die. This is a hard idea to accept, but one should not dismiss it too quickly. Islamists are happy to die in the pursuit of their objectives because as martyrs they are honored and welcomed by God. Death in the pursuit of jihad is to be celebrated.

Although Saudi Arabia has recently moved to seek relationships with Israel it is new and tentative. It remains to be seen how this develops. This Hamas / Gaza conflict obviously delays any rapprochement.

More-Moderate Muslim Nations

As we move further away from Iran and Saudi Arabia to other Islam regions we find various degrees of evolution from the theocratic state model to more secular and tolerant societies. In the Middle East and South East Europe Albania, Turkey, Azerbaijan, Tajikistan, Kazakhstan and Jordan come to mind. In North Africa Egypt, Tunisia, Morocco and Algeria qualify. In Asia Pakistan, Bangladesh, Malaysia and Indonesia also qualify. I am ignoring the small Gulf countries because they are small and operate more like city states. There is reason to be hopeful that given time these fourteen countries can continue to develop so that citizens who are not Muslims can have equal rights and respect. Having said that the challenges for these hopeful countries are immense. The problem is the power of the Mullahs. Without a clear separation of state and mosque there is no chance. Let's examine a recent situation in Pakistan.

In Pakistan in 2016 the ruling Muslim League party was moving toward passing legislation that would have raised the legal age of marriage to eighteen. The current status was that girls as young as nine years old were eligible to marry as long as the signs of puberty were visible. What happened? What happened is that the country's Council of Islamic Ideology declared that such a law was contrary to the teachings of Muhammad and that to pass it would be blasphemous. Now acts of blasphemy can be punishable by death. Consequently the proposed Child Marriage Restraint Bill was killed. Such is the power of Islam in these countries. One of Pakistan's challenges is that Islam is the official religion of the country. Given that, can they ever escape from the control of the mullahs? Can they ever put in place a structure that would allow free enterprise to flourish and that would respect broader concepts of human rights and genuine respect for persons of other religions? There are persons in Pakistan who would like to go in such a direction, but with the ability of the mullahs to play the blasphemy card, one must question if it will ever happen. Such are the challenges of Islam.

However, even if such structural progress were possible in these countries, there remains very significant cultural discontinuities between how a Muslim family functions and how a Christian family operates.

Christians view their religion as a foundation to pursue their interests in the world. Certainly for a Protestant Christian, there is no one between a person and God. Contrastingly, Muslims are taught that the purpose of life is to worship the Prophet Muhammed and follow all of his teachings. These are fundamentally different viewpoints, and they shape how individuals prioritize their activities. Additionally, Muslims have the possible controlling influence of an imam or mullah to deal with. It is difficult to make generalized statements about Islam or Muslims. There are both more liberal and conservative branches of Islam. The Islamic community can be sorted into four separate groups. These are as follows:

Theocratic expansionists (about 5 percent, 80 million)

This is the Muslim Brotherhood, al-Qaeda, ISIS, Hamas, Hezbollah, Taliban, Boko Haram, Al- Shabab, Ansar al-Sharia, Jemaah Islamiah and their hidden supporters. If you want the blessing of Allah to go release your bestial instincts, then this is where you belong.

Islamists (about 36 percent, 576 million)

These are extra-pious Muslims who faithfully and dogmatically follow the Koran, including sharia law. This category includes most of the clergy (mullahs, imams, et al.), who have a great influence on the mass of ordinary Muslims. These are the proponents of Islamic theocracies. Saudi Arabia and Iran are both theocracies.

Ordinary Muslims (about 56 percent, 896 million)

These people just want to get on with their life and take care of their family while being good Muslims.

Muslims in name only (MINOs) (about 3 percent, 48 million)

These are Muslims who have crossed over and now embrace mainstream Western values, but they find themselves stuck. To walk away from Islam is apostasy, which carries the possible penalty of death depending on where you live. So these people remain Muslims in theory, but they live by Western values.

I believe it is appropriate to view the theocratic expansionists and the Islamists as being in a separate category from the Ordinary Muslims and the MINO's. Let's call the theocratic expansionists and the Islamists the "Islam Rules" group. The Islam Rules group see Islam as a way to organize practically every aspect of society. Saudi Arabia was probably the best example of Islam Rules. Islam is the only religion allowed there. The laws of the land are the laws of the Koran, namely, sharia law. The financial system comports to the Koran's ban on usury. Family life and social interactions are quite tightly ruled. The role of men versus the role of women is defined. Women are under the control of men in every aspect of their existence. There are proscribed dress codes. The imams have immense power over their followers. There are religious police who roam the streets to ensure that the citizens behave. This brand of Islam is much more than a religion. It is a system for organizing society, but only for Muslims. Non-Muslims are only tolerated if they serve a purpose. Westerners need to take a step back and understand what they are dealing with. With Islam Rules, it is not a question of religious tolerance; it is a question of a whole way of life that conflicts with Western values and culture in so many ways. Having said all that I must note that Saudi Arabia is trying to move away from its strict "wahabi" controlled culture. It is embryonic but encouraging.

With ordinary Muslims and MINOs, we are dealing with something that more closely resembles religion as a personal choice. With such people, there is a chance that they could assimilate into a Western culture. There remain major challenges, both cultural and regarding taught beliefs, but there is a chance.

Turkey is a successful example of what is possible. Turkey is a secular democracy with a constitution guaranteeing the separation of mosque and state. As a result of the First World War, the Ottoman Empire was broken up. Following this there was a War of Independence in Turkey, and in 1922 the sultanate was replaced by the modern secular Republic of Turkey. Mustafa Kemal Atatürk (Father of the Turks) led Turkey in the war. He is viewed as the father of the current Republic of Turkey. Over the years the military has occasionally been required to step in and enforce the constitution, similar to the history in Egypt. However, from a capitalism viewpoint, Turkey, with its thirty-two billionaires, eight of whom are women, is doing well.

The problem that the leaders of the fourteen hopeful Muslim countries have is that while they try to modernize their countries, they have, to varying degrees, radical Muslim citizens and radical imams and mullahs that they must deal with. Balanced against the fourteen Muslim countries that are in the hopeful category, there are thirty-two Muslim majority countries that at this time are hopeless—hopeless because of their combination of Islamic governments, poverty, illiteracy, and limited economic empowerment. Last, we have Iran and Saudi Arabia. Iran is unmoving because of its theocratic control and Saudi Arabia is trying to join the modern world.

The Future

The future of the Middle East will be determined by the future policies of Iran, Saudi Arabia, Turkey, and Egypt. The West has a role to play in influencing these policies. Turkey is the best example of a modern Muslim-majority state. Its current leader, Erdoğan, has been disassembling the good work of Atatürk. He has attacked and weakened the military. He has corrupted the independence of the judiciary. He has weakened the independence of the press. He is an Islamist. Turkey, a NATO member and on the cusp of European Union membership, is turning away from all the progress it has made since 1923. Fortunately the Turkish public seems to be getting tired of 65% inflation and in the recent provincial elections they voted for change

Iran has a population that includes many people from before the revolution in 1979 who have pro-Western views. However, 1979 was forty-five years ago. It is inevitable that those people's influence on current affairs is fading. The reality is that the radical Islamists are in power and they are not afraid to use their power to stay in power. One of the ways that the religious leaders do this is by exercising their power to approve all the candidates that stand for election to parliament. Based on the writings and speeches of the current leader, Ayatollah Khamenei, the desire to destroy Israel is very real and persistent.

Egypt is important because of its population (one hundred and fourteen million) and what used to be the close alliance between the military (which controls the country) and the United States. Barack Obama and Hillary Clinton put it all at risk by abandoning President Mubarak and enabling the Muslim Brotherhood to get control. Thankfully, Egypt is back on track with General el-Sisi in control. God bless him. Egypt and Jordan are the only two Arab allies that Israel currently has.

Saudi Arabia is the country that can determine the future of radical Islam and the Middle East. Saudi Arabia was the major sponsor of Salafism, which is the most conservative brand of Sunni Islam. Most of the radical Islamic organizations originate from Saudi Arabia. Saudi Arabia is a state with strong theocratic sharia law. Saudi Arabia is the ultimate family business.

CHAPTER 3.3

HEY- LET'S TAX THE RICH MORE

INCOME TAX RATES AND GOVERNMENT REVENUES

In the United States, the issue of the top 1 percent income earners is now very political. It falls under the "inequality" label, and the assumption is that too much inequality is bad. This is a Democratic party issue. It is the soft headed "Robin Hood " heritage……..let's steal from the rich and give to the poor. It is the basic thought underlying most marxist/socialist thinking. Venezuela which has some of the largest oil reserves in the world tried this by nationalizing their oil and gas industry in 1976. Within 20 years they were in trouble and today they are a total mess with their citizens fleeing to Columbia and to the USA.

Hey! the Democrats say we only want to take a little. Today in the USA the income tax contributions are as follows (2020 data):

The top 1% of earners contribute 45.8% of total tax revenue.
The top 50% of earners contribute 97.7% of total tax revenue.
The bottom 50% of earners contribute 2.3% of total tax revenue.

Now we have a lot of very rich people in the USA so the feeling is surely they could pay a little more. However, history shows us that GDP growth is more important in driving government tax revenues than the marginal tax rate. Over the last 70 years the US top marginal tax rate has varied from as high as 91% to a low of 28% (it is presently 37%). During that time the government tax revenues expressed as a percentage of GDP have always been in the 16-20% range. So clearly what the top marginal tax rate is not the most important variable in influencing the government's revenue.

The most important objective is to maximize GDP. When it comes to maximizing GDP the best thing the government can do is to get out of the way and help the functioning of free markets. The current Biden initiatives to sponsor electrical car manufacturing, restrict oil and gas, promote semiconductor plants, improve insulation in housing and more will end badly. It would be more helpful to reduce regulations, speed up approval times for permits for major infrastructure programs, etc. These are just a few ideas.

If you can get GDP growing faster everyone wins because there are more jobs and wages will increase as companies compete for labor. Hey we might even be able to reduce the number of federal employees which is presently 2.87 million.

The other important thought is the government needs to live within its means. As we have discovered since 2019 when the government spends more than it brings in the risk is inflation. Inflation destroys income gains. We cannot prevent some of our citizens running up their credit card debt but we do not need the government doing the same thing.

What we need is a virtuous cycle……less government spending and less regulations leading to higher GDP growth leading to more people working leading to reduced government spending to help our poorest citizens and so on. This is not just a fiscal issue it will help raise people out of dependency on the government and give them purpose and pride.

WEALTH AND CAPITAL

Today there is about 25 million millionaires in the USA. The number of millionaires in the world is estimated at 60 million. There is about 2800 billionaires in the world with a total net worth of $14 trillion. Amazingly China has the most billionaires at 814. Gee this communist gig is fun particularly if you are a friend of President Xi. When I look at these numbers it all kind of seems obscene. Gee how much money does a guy need? Now I am using guy for convenience, 383 of the billionaires are women, apologies.

However, that is dumb thinking. The way to think about it is that these millionaires and billionaires are like the gas stations that provide the fuel(capital) for our capital system to function. Many of them are wealthy because of businesses they created and much of their money is still tied up in their business. I bet that many of them have invested capital in other startup ventures. And the rest is invested in public equities or hedge funds. They are capitalists and capital is what creates economic growth, creates technical innovation and what makes the stock market and your 401 plan go up.

The thing you have to think about is whether you would rather these guys choose where to invest their capital or would you rather have the government confiscate some of their wealth and invest it in what? I say invest but it is more likely the correct word is SPEND.

If you are having trouble buying what I am selling here do not feel bad. It just means you do not understand how this capitalism thing works. I explained it in chapter 3.1 so go back and do a review. Do not feel bad. We just do not teach this stuff. It should be a requirement that before you graduate from high school you should have a CIVICS class explaining how the your government is structured and a class on free market capitalism starting with the teachings of my fellow Scot, Adam Smith, the author of "Wealth of Nations" published in 1776 just about the time that the embryonic USA was looking for inspiration. What a coincidence!

CHAPTER 4.1

WE THE PEOPLE VERSUS THEY THE GOVERNMENT

Coming out of the Second World War, people felt a great relief that the killing had ended. The United States was able to switch its war manufacturing capacity to peaceful uses, and as a result its economy started to surge. Life was good. In Europe the damage and dislocation of persons and infrastructure was significant. This delayed events but by the 1950's Europe was also experiencing an economic recovery. In both cases the growing economy brought prosperity to the people in the sixties. On the foreign policy front, the focus was the Cold War with the communist Soviet Republic and, to a lesser extent, China. This remained a stable situation up until the eighties. During this time, the governments in the United States and Europe put in place the fairly complete welfare programs that we enjoy today. Part of the prosperity bonus was the expansion of university education to a broader social spectrum. Four factors came together in the sixties and seventies in the United States, as follows:

The presence on campuses of a much broader social spectrum: more women, more minorities, more of all sorts of people. This led to a social awakening. All of this contributed to a counterculture of feminists, gay activists, Black Panthers, drug experimentation and hippies.

Civil rights. In the sixties television confronted many people who lived in the North with the segregation and injustices visited on the black population in the South. The Civil Rights legislation of 1964 was necessary and overdue. Following this was the Great Society welfare legislation of President Johnson in 1965. Johnson's welfare reform penalized two parent families to the advantage of single parent families. Since then we have seen in the northern cities of the USA the destruction of the black family and a failure by black Democratic Mayors to provide adequate education opportunities to their black citizens.

The birth control pill. We should not blame all of the increased sexuality of US society on birth control pills, but the pill certainly was an ingredient that along with drugs and no-fault divorce fueled a hedonistic culture. This was the sex, drugs, and rock and roll culture, which, while sounding trendy, was really destructive.

The Vietnam War. The war was the trigger for the antiauthority, "let's change the world" movement. The young people in the late sixties had been brought up to respect authority. The Vietnam War led to increasing protests. Protests were against university presidents, the government, and the army. When the protestors won, they felt empowered to go on and challenge all authority. The progressive ideology got its start in 1969 with some universities agreeing to create some chairs in Africa American Studies. Women studies followed and then gender studies fueling the grievance industry that we have today. Many of the protestors, and even some terrorists, from that time gravitated, as they got older, into education, into government, and into the nonprofit segments of our society, still pursuing their ideals from their protest days. These ideals include a negative view of US foreign policy because of the Vietnam War and more recently the Iraq War. These people believe that the attitudes of the white heterosexual majority are a problem. This is the white supremacy charge. They hold the view that the historical sins of Western civilization have to be atoned for, that US society is unjust and discriminatory. Over the last 50 years many of these " let's change the world" ideologues have risen to powerful positions in government and especially our universities. How is that working out?

Money Talks. In recent times we have seen very significant foreign funds contributed to US universities. Between 1986 and 2022 about $44 billion has been contributed. About $11 billion came from the Middle East with Qatar, Saudi Arabia and the UAE being the biggest donors. This has resulted in multiple chairs in Palestinian Studies being established and in addition there is over 200 chapters of Students for Justice in Palestine on US campuses. The recent uprisings on US campuses supporting Hamas are a direct result of this influence on the US university system. What is it that these university presidents do not understand. Palestine (Arafat) had opportunities in the past to make peace and move on. They chose not to. These universities should return the "blood money" and turn away from these terrorist front organizations.

In the same time period China has established over 100 Confucius Institutes in US universities and over 500 in K1-K12 school classrooms. These institutes are in most matters directly funded and controlled by the Chinese. One can assume that these institutes present a favorable view of Chinese culture. It is estimated that Chinese students in the US contribute $12 billion a year in tuition. Many of these students are studying and working in high technology fields. The PRC for the last 50 years has been stealing our technology by hacking and forcing companies into joint ventures. Having their citizens work in our high technology organizations is just another way for them to steal our technology. What is it that these university presidents do not understand.

China is not interested in win-win. China is interested in China wins the USA loses. In addition their human rights record is atrocious as to their own people but also to the Uyghurs.

These are the same university Presidents that require faculty applying for a position to write something explaining how they support Diversity Equity and Inclusion (DEI). Talk about thought orthodoxy! No wonder they like the PRC and President Xi.

The contrasting reality was all the folks who did not protest the Vietnam War and who did not go to university. These were the folks who did go, and fight and die (58220 deaths) in the Vietnam War and were reviled when they returned. These are the folks who got up every morning and went to work. If that was not enough, in the following thirty years these were the folks who lost their good-paying union jobs in the clothing mills, in the shoe factories, in the steel mills and in the automotive plants as the United States innovated and started to have to compete globally.

More recently, these are the same folks who have continued to suffer because of increased legal and, especially, illegal immigration. Now the media are trying to figure out who are all the people supporting Donald

Trump. The answer is the suppressed working folks who have found a champion who is willing to take on the educated elite who have dominated the national stage for the last fifty years.

So today in America we have real divisions in our society. We have an elite who only see the shortcomings of America. This elite is suspicious of the American power structure and its role as a leader in the world. This elite does not believe in American exceptionalism. This elite has effectively limited free speech in their pursuit of social justice. Their social justice vision includes white supremacy, LGBTQIA2S+, equity, transgenderism, social pronouns, ESG, DEI and more. Opposed to this view are a lot of folks who are totally bamboozled by this continuing avalanche of issues that impact less than 6% of the population. The folks are not unsympathetic to some of these issues, but their beef is let's focus on what is important to the 94% of us who are heterosexual. The title of this chapter, "We the People versus They the Government," captures the mood of the United States today. In the United States there still is a strong belief in the meaning of the phrase we the people in the Constitution. There is a feeling that the freedom to be and act on your individual beliefs is slipping away. That is partly why many people support Donald Trump. The objective is to put a people's representative in charge in Washington to try and solve practical problems and not pursue ideological marginal issues.

In Europe, the governments have already taken over a larger part of the economy, but I give the Europeans credit. They are not so attracted to these fringe social issues. However, they are trapped in a reality of high taxes to support high government spending. Here is some data:

TABLE Government Expenditures as % of GDP

	Germany	France	Italy	UK	USA
Tax burden as % of GDP	47.1	53.6	48.8	38.9	33
Expenditure as % of GDP	49.7	58.5	56.8	45.1	38.5

In Europe there is a bigger social welfare-network than in the USA. But life is a zero-sum game. The tradeoff is that the business sector is less vibrant because of higher taxes. This means there is less economic growth. And that means fewer opportunities for young people. As Europe moved into the seventies, the mission of creating a closer and more perfect union of the countries in Europe picked up speed. In the beginning there were clear benefits, but over time, as the union expanded and the powers of the European Commission grew, the people began to feel a loss of control over their own sovereign affairs. Over time it seems that more and more key decisions for the European Union are negotiated behind closed doors by a small group of representatives, with Germany having the biggest say. The increasing concentration of power in the European Commission, the effects of Muslim immigration, and the European Monetary Union are the three drivers of disaffection in Europe.

How We Got Here: Europe

Europe was just getting back on its feet after the Second World War. The amount of psychological scar tissue in Europe was immense. This scar tissue reflected an immense amount of guilt and horror, particularly in France and Germany, considering what they had done in the First and Second World Wars. Let's list some of the horrifying facts.

First World War

French persons killed: 1.7 million (4.3 percent of population)
German persons killed: 2.8 million (4.3 percent of population)
Total number killed: 18 million

Second World War

French persons killed: 600,000 (1.4 percent of population)
German persons killed: 5.7 million (8.2 percent of population)

Holocaust deaths: 12.7 million (6 million Jews, but also Communists, Jehovah's Witnesses, Gypsies, homosexuals, and others). In the Second World War, France was divided into the German occupied part and the

French managed part (Vichy, France), the latter of which cooperated with the Nazis in rounding up Jews.

Total number killed: 85 million throughout Europe and Asia

That is a total of 103 million people killed in only 31 years (1914 to 1945).

So given this history, what did the French and Germans do? They decided that they had to rush toward each other and embrace one another so tightly that such a great loss of life could never happen again. It started with creating a single steel market in 1951 and went from there, one step at a time moving more and more toward a fully integrated and larger Europe. The early steps were very positive. The elimination of border controls leading to the creation of a free single market and freedom of movement was a very positive step and whetted the appetite for more.

Once there was European politicians and a governing structure the trend to expanding and more closely integrating the countries in the Union was unstoppable. There were some skeptics.

Margaret Thatcher was one. She kept the United Kingdom out of adopting the euro. Then in 2020 the UK formally withdrew from the European Union. Today the European Union includes 27 countries, 20 of which use the euro as their currency.

Serious opposition to the ever expanding, ever more perfect European Union started to develop on the right sometime around the year 2000, largely in resistance to the cultural issues around Muslim immigration. In the press, these new political parties are usually referred to as Far Right political parties, which, coming from the media, is not meant as a compliment. They are far right in so far as the socialists are far left. What they stand for, in general, is the right to maintain their culture and have more local control. In this affirmative statement is a rejection of the immigration of persons who in some proportion do not want to assimilate. When you live in a time period when cultural diversity is a minor god, such attitudes are viewed as primitive and regressive. I do not think they are primitive and regressive. A nation is built by the hard work of the folks. The folks are entitled to be proud of their country and protect it's cultural norms.. The question of putting limits on immigration into Europe and North America is not if; it is when.

Also, it is not a Muslim issue alone. There are many non-Muslim people who want to come to the United States and Europe to live. Considering all of this, we have seen the rapid growth of right wing parties in Europe that have a variety of issues on their agenda, but common to them all is the concern about immigration and, in particular Muslim immigration.

How We Got Here: The United States

The US story is simpler than Europe's. The US federal structure has always existed. At the founding of the union the power resided with the states. Today it resides in Washington, DC. What really got this trend rolling was the activity in the 1960s on civil rights and the Great Society welfare legislation. In the last fifty years, the federal government's revenue has grown rapidly, and so has its spending habits. The federal government uses its funds to force state governments to implement many policies so that we get one size fits all government in many areas. That this has occurred is unfortunate, because one of the great potential strengths of America is the diversity of cultures in the states. For a long time in the United States, everything was fine. It was fine because the US economy grew consistently at a rate that gave us the wealth to afford all the new federal programs and their accompanying bureaucracies. The United States is now paying for all these wonderful programs by going deeper and deeper into debt ($37 trillion and growing). Practically everyone understands that we need to reform our entitlement programs and that we need to get the economy growing at a higher rate. Ilegal immigration is probably closer to 35 million than to the 11 million the government and media continually quote. Recent persistant inflation because of the excessive COVID spending, the electrical vehicle subsidies, the student loan forgiveness and more has the working folks struggling and disgruntled. We also know that the destruction of traditional families, especially in black communities, is partly the result of how our welfare programs are designed. The Democrats' solution to the low growth economy is to further redistribute the wealth with no realistic policies directed at getting the pie to grow bigger and faster. Donald Trump in his first term was quite successful in promoting the economy and enhancing working folks incomes. It is hard to know what he would do in a second term but I would guess that he would for starters shut down the entry of illegal immigrants and move back to supporting oil and gas.

Experimental, Incremental Change versus Visionary Hoped-for Change

The intellectual elite in media, in academia, and in government never get fired because they deal only in ideas and have no responsibility for outcomes. Many of these people are in the business of shouting "fire" in a crowded cinema. They seek to be noticed and sought out. There you have the divide between evolutionary incremental change and the grand vision. The grand vision of the intellectuals is of a global cooperative community with open borders and similar values. It sounds great. The problem is that apart from Europe and the United States, the world did not get the memo. The reality in the world today is that nations act in their naked self-interest to the disadvantage of others. Allow me to give you a few examples:

Russia takes over control of Crimea......2014

North Korea ignores threats and warnings to discontinue its nuclear and ballistic missile programs.

Iran sponsors terrorism, pursues nuclear bomb technology, develops ballistic missile capability, takes hostages as negotiating currency, and pursues a Shia hegemony, and gets rewarded by Obama and now Biden.

China occupies South China Sea Islands, builds airports on them, and places missile defenses on them despite the protests of many nations, especially the Phillipines.

ISIS kills Jews and Christians only because of their faith or, if the females are Christians, the operatives of ISIS take them as sex slaves.

Hezbollah and Hamas continuously fire rockets into Israel

Syrian civil war.

Russia invades Ukraine.

China continually menaces Taiwan.

China acts to eliminate the Uyghers and suppress the Nepalese people.

Yemen Houthis fire rockets into Saudi Arabia and more recently the Red Sea.

Turkey and Iran continue to persecute the Kurds.

Hamas attack Israel from Gaza.

Iran attempts to demolish Israel.

Saudi Arabia versus Iran in Yemen and Syria.

All the above does not include the mayhem in Sub-Sahara Africa and the Sudan/Somalia conflicts.

The vision that all the nations of the world and all the tribes of the world and all the religions of the world can live in peace does not square with reality. Many of the citizens of Europe and the United States see this gap between the way the world is versus the way their political leaders would like it to be. These differences create in people an alienation from and a distrust of their leaders. This distrust is increased because over the last forty years the intellectuals have cried wolf over and over and have been proven wrong. What the working folks want is not visionary leaders but practical people who can protect the nation and make government more efficient.

Very Smart People and Their Speculative Ideas

The intellectual elite who dominate the media, politics, and academia are quite certain about their world vision. This is a little scary, because their track record is not good. Over the last seventy years they have made and promoted a number of predictions, all of which have been false.. Let's review a few.

We Will Not Have Enough Food and Water

The concern was that with the continuing growth in the world's population, there would not be enough food and water for everyone. This was a popular idea back in the sixties and seventies. It turns out that the world has more than ample capability to feed the world. Where there are pockets of hunger in the world, this is the result of distribution problems, which are usually exacerbated by local insecurity and government corruption. South Sudan is a current example of this. If Sudan were at peace and the basic institutions of a government were working, then getting food to the people would be quite possible.

Clean, abundant water is a requirement of life. In certain parts of the world, it is a challenge to find clean water, and with a growing population it will become more of a challenge. One answer lies in taking seawater and using reverse osmosis desalinization plants to turn it into clean drinking water. Yes, you need electricity to do this, so the water costs more. The technology to do this has been developed by the Israelis and is readily available. The Israelis are also able to recycle most of their wastewater in creative ways. Cities like Singapore are also using reverse osmosis to recycle wastewater. As long as we plan ahead, water should never be a problem.

Peak Oil and Energy Alternatives

For decades it was consistently predicted that oil production was about to peak and then decline. This was the "peak oil" prediction. Today it is obvious that for the indeterminate future, there is plenty of oil and gas in the world. It is just a matter of the cost to produce and distribute it.

Nuclear Power

Nuclear power provides almost an infinite supply of energy and is also the most environmentally benign way to generate electricity. But the greenies are afraid of it The nation that has embraced nuclear power the most is

France. About 76 percent of France's electricity is generated by nuclear power, and much of the rest is from hydroelectric power created by having the nuclear plants, in off-peak hours, pump water up mountains. Despite the fact that nuclear power is the most carbon friendly energy source the environmentalists are afraid of it and have been shutting it down. They only embraced nuclear power for the first time at the most recent Global Climate Conference in Dubai in 2024.

Global Warming, aka Climate Change

When the president of the United States says that climate change is the single biggest risk to the United States it gets everyone's attention. The issue correctly stated is whether humanity's activities on earth are enhancing global warming to such a degree that we need significant changes in public policy to curb carbon dioxide production in order to avoid significant negative environmental impacts.

Here are my concerns:

We know the earth is in a warming cycle. It then becomes very difficult to separate the underlying warming from any additional warming due to the additional carbon dioxide added by humans.

It is admitted that whatever carbon dioxide reductions the US and Europe can achieve will do very little to reduce the overall carbon dioxide increases because they are small compared to what China, India and the developing world are pumping out.

So instead of spending a lot of money in the USA to reduce CO_2 emissions which will have very little worldwide impact would we not be better spending our funds on how to remove CO_2 from the atmosphere using new initiatives like sequestering?

Aditionally I would feel a lot better if someone could explain to me why the earth has been both cooling and heating for 100's of thousands of years. I have researched this enigma and apart from some hand waving generalities there are no convincing answers.

I would suggest that this is a case of the "very smart people" over hyping something and the rest of the world playing along in a shakedown of the USA and Europe to their own benefit. It looks like a classic case of "the king has no clothes".

Why Do Smart People Consistently Get It Wrong?

Predicting the future will always be difficult. The history of the last fifty years shows that people continue to get it wrong. Here are four reasons why this happens:

Predicting that everything is fine does not generate interest, get you published, or get you research funds. There is a significant bias to push ideas that are popular. As a result science becomes very political as opposed to objective fact driven.

Underestimating technology – The reason humanity has advanced in the last 240 years is technology. There is a reasonable chance we can solve most problems we confront with new technical innovations. Many of the people making these predictions have little understanding of our technological capability.

Crony capitalism – Corporations with a vested interest, supported by ideas people with a vested interest, persuade lawmakers that they need to subsidize in some way a new technology for the future benefit of the nation. This is self-interest manipulating the ignorant. Ethanol, solar power, wind turbines, and electric vehicles all come to mind.

The Drivers of Opposition Today

There are economic challenges and cultural challenges. After seventy-five years of go-along, get-along centrist political policies, the party is over. We are seeing new political parties emerge in Europe on the right that are challenging the centrist parties for power. The center is losing support. One action that would be helpful is to move more power away from these central governments and return it to the states and member countries, where differentiated policies can be crafted that are more responsive to the local realities. California is quite different from Texas. Portugal, Greece, and Hungary are quite different from Germany. The folks want solutions customized to their local situation, not one size fits all. We need to find a way to retain the economic advantages of large homogeneous markets and coordinated foreign policies while delegating everything else to the most local level possible. The changes that are needed are much easier to implement in the United States because of the Federal State structure. The European Union has a greater dilemma. The reasons behind the growing rebellion against big government can be placed into two buckets. One is economic, and the other is cultural.

Economic Bucket

Real wage growth is not keeping up with inflation.

Legal and illegal immigration suppresses the cost of labor.

Automation also reduces labor demand. Is "AI" next?

Globalization reduces the number of jobs in manufacturing in the United States and Europe.

Poor education hampers employment participation for some.

Cultural Bucket

There are two competing cultures in Europe and the United States. One is the wealth-creation culture, and the other is the wealth-redistribution culture.

The wealth-creation culture is the private business sector. It is fundamentally a meritocracy. A meritocratic culture is built around the idea that individuals all have an equal opportunity to participate in society. They do not necessarily have an equal chance, because, as described earlier, individuals are a product of the family they are born into. In that sense, life at its start is profoundly unfair. This culture does well in environments where performance is highly valued and measured. So it generally does well in free market conditions, such as businesses and professional sports. This part of the economy operates 24/7 and is efficient. If you are not efficient, then you will not survive.

The wealth-redistribution culture consists of all of government plus the beneficiaries of the government's spending and subsidies. Consequently, all colleges, maybe to their surprise, are in the wealth-redistribution game. I say this because the government student loan program is the main reason college tuition has risen at a rate far more than inflation. Practically all of the health care industry and all the pharmaceutical industry is indirectly government controlled. These parts of the economy are inefficient and depend on government spending and regulations.

It is a little bit of a stretch, but you can theorize that the wealth-creation culture is primarily the culture from which the folks who support Trump come. These folks work in private businesses and want good paying jobs. They understand that we need policies that will create higher GDP growth. When you look at the policies of Biden/Harris they are heavily biased towards government intervention in what should be free markets. Examples are the Inflation Reduction Act, student loans forgiveness, restrictions on oil and gas exploration and distribution of oil and gas, semiconductor subsidies.

The United States is a country that is splitting apart in the pursuit of two entirely different visions. Most of the political debate is about economic issues. Although these economic issues are important, I believe a big part of the opposition is the loss of credibility of the intellectual elite and a resistance to the assumptions they make about the culture in the United States and Europe. Their ideas and policies just do not pass the commonsense test for many voters.

Material Wealth versus Values

What good does it do you to inherit the riches of the world if in so doing you lose your soul? In many ways, this question captures the Judeo-Christian dilemma. Over the last forty years the West has become richer and richer, as measured by GDP per capita. At the same time, Western culture has become more and more vulgar, and disrespectful of life. This has been a slow process, but the trend has been in one direction and it offends the Judeo-Christian values of many.

The biggest business on the Internet is pornography. Porn gives young people the wrong impression of sex and of the male–female relationship. Cold-blooded killing with no remorse seems to happen more often, particularly in the United States. Every day there is another case of teachers, usually female, indulging themselves by having sex with underage children in their care. More and more children grow up in single-parent homes (30 percent in the United States), and more of these kids have problems than those in two-parent families. Our entertainment figures (e.g., Madonna, Lady Gaga, Miley Cyrus, and the Kardashians) have found that the way to get noticed is to flout as much tits and ass as possible. Drug use is widespread. Transgender surgeries? LGBTQIA2S+? DEI? ESG?......it goes on and on and many voters are befuddled by it all.

Many people are unhappy with these changes and resist them. The societal issue is the remaining folks who live their lives based on the role models they see. These are not healthy role models for society. This is the challenge for the West: the need to become a more value-driven culture and to strengthen the role of the two-parent family.

Interestingly, Muslim countries seem in some ways to be the reverse of the West. They have strong family structures but have difficulty delivering economic prosperity. If you visit Muslim sites such as www.missionmuslim.com it is clear that Muslims understand this difference and are certain that the choice they are making are better than those made in the West. The migration of Muslims to the West gives them access to the West's prosperity, but to protect their family structure they need to insulate themselves from the depravities of the West by creating separate communities. This is why you see the pressure from Muslims to have their own schools, and sharia courts for family law. This is why assimilation can be so difficult. Many Muslims correctly see assimilation as destructive to their family rules, ethics, and practices.

The Organized Opposition

Politics in Europe and the United States are changing. The centrist political parties are being challenged by new parties on the right. Here is the status:

In Europe

Netherlands: In Nov 2023 Geert Wilders leader of the antimuslim immigration party got the most votes with 23.5% competing against 15 parties.

Greece: In June 2023 The New Democracy, which leans right, won the election.

Switzerland: In October 2023, the right-wing Swiss People's Party, receives 28 percent of the popular vote which is the largest out of 10 parties. The Swiss People's Party seeks to control immigration.

Poland: In April 2022, the United Right Party (which is opposed to immigration) wins 35 percent of the vote but was unable to form a new government.

Hungary: Viktor Orbán, the current prime minister who is against the Muslim refugee deluge, was overwhelmingly reelected to his fourth term as Prime Minister. Orban has been consistently anti-immigration and pro-family.

France: In April 2022 Marine Le Pen significantly increased her share of the vote at 41.4% and was second to Macron. This continued improving support for the National Rally party is consistent with the continuing and escalating problems France has with Muslims.

Germany: The Alternative for Germany (AfD) party was founded in 2013 to demand more economic discipline in Europe. It has morphed to now represent the anti-refugee sentiment in Germany. In the 2021 elections it receive 10.4% of the vote.

Italy: In September 2022 the Brother's of Italy won the greatest share of the vote and Giorga Meloni was elected Prime Minister.

Note: To Americans, some of these shares of the vote in Europe may seem small. However, in Europe there are many more political parties and most governments are based on coalitions. These election movements to the right continued in the June 2024 European parliament elections.

The general overall trend in European politics is that the right wing, anti-Muslim immigration parties that first started to be created about 2000 have moved into the mainstream. Their challenge in continuing to grow is that some of the larger historical parties have been nudged to be more anti-immigrant and at the same time the new anti-immigrant parties in turn need to broaden their agenda to attract more voters. Not surprisingly we see the biggest movement in the Netherlands and France, two countries who have experienced many Muslim incidents.

In the United States

In the 2020 election process the Democratic party presented itself as a steadying hand. Since being elected, Biden has enabled increased illegal immigration, been weak in dealing with Afghanistan and Iran, committed the USA to an energy transition on an unrealistic timetable, forgiven oodles of student debt, undercut Israel, to name some of his initiatives. The actions of Joe Biden after 2020 have felt like a betrayal to some traditional democrats. The bottom line is that both the Republican party and the Democrat party have new positions. What has changed?

The new DEMOCRATIC party is:

It is the green party/anti fossil fuels & gas\electric vehicle mandates etc.
It is the pro illegal immigration party
It is the apologist for its conservative Muslim wing
It is "who cares about tomorrow" party……national debt, entitlement reform
It is the progressive party: white supremacy, DEI, transgenderism, etc.
It is LGBTQIA2S+
It is in favor of abortion up to the time of birth.

It is ideological

The new REPUBLICAN party is:

Pro American manufacturing
Pro our oil & gas industry
It is anti all illegal immigration
It does not fear confronting Putin, Xi and Khamenei
It is pro traditional American values
It believes that there are only two sexes…..male and female
It accepts States' right to establish reasonable abortion limits……..15 or 18 weeks
It is pragmatic

It takes time for the voting public to react to these changes. A large section of the voting public is born into a political party and these loyalties used to last until death. What happens, however, when your party fundamentally changes. It takes time for the voting public to make up its mind about these new parties based on what they do. We now have one outing for Trump, 2016-2020 and one outing for Biden 2020-2024 and one outing for Obama, 2012-2016. Voters are weighing what they see and have experienced. November 2024 will give us an update on what our fellow citizens think.

GLOBAL POLITICS

I am talking about the United Nations, the World Health Organization and their ilk. These organizations provide an opportunity for grandstanding and little else. They cannot agree on anything that matters. The best you can say for them is that they provide a good venue for exchanging opposed opinions

CHAPTER 4.2

CAN GOVERNMENTS RESPOND?

The USA

When the Founders of what was to become the US were in Philadelphia negotitaing "the deal" to come together for mutual defense and a unified foreign policy they each wanted to retain the freedom to manage their own states separately and individually. This is the "Federation of States" that makes up the United States of America.

This mechanism has been a wonderful vehicle for the US to evolve over time towards a shared value system particularly on the treatment of minorities. Within the USA there are states that are growing, states that have a stable population and states that are losing population. These population shifts are caused by many factors but one of them is the different policies of the state governments. Just looking at state tax rates you have California with a marginal tax rate of 12.3% as compared to 9 states with no income tax. There are also many other differences on social policy issues. The differences between Florida and California are dramatic and it is clear that the majority of the voters prefer Florida. Voters are fleeing the big democratic states such as Illinois, New York and California for Republican states such as Texas, Florida and Tennessee. These choices by the electorate and businesses are democracy functioning by action. By moving they send a message to the state they live in at the same time rewarding the state with the policies they prefer. The movement in people from state-to-state results in changes in the number of congressmen each state has which over time influences federal policies. The net effect is that the USA has a system that is responsive to the choices people make in judging different state government policies. Recent history is that voters have been leaving Democrat controlled states to go to Republican controlled states.

Europe

Europe is a parliamentary form of government which means you only get one set of policies for about four years. Then you get another chance for another four years. Unfortunately, it is worse than that because most governments are coalitions so as a voter you can never really predict what the policies of your coalition government will be. The policies will reflect the issues of the parties that make up the coalition. The result is that European countries are limited in the speed at which they can respond to emerging issues.

CHAPTER 5

THE FOUR THUGS

A dictionary definition of a thug is a violent, lawless, or vicious person, especially one who commits a crime such as assault, robbery, or murder. Such people obviously have issues that allow them to be cruel to others, possibly because they have had earlier painful experiences. Such thugs find out as they progress that they can prevail because their fellow human beings are not willing to confront their demands. The thug gets used to using his power to get his way.

Most of us have little experience of this behavior. The example in the USA that you might understand is when the big kid approaches another kid and demands that he hand over his lunch money. If the smaller kid complies the thug comes back the next week and does it again. This is bullying.

It can happen between nations. Some of the global leaders we confront have got to their positions by intrigue and power plays. In contrast many of our highly educated diplomats went to affluent schools where all disputes are mediated. They never had to confront a real bully growing up.

They never learn the visceral skills of assessing an opponent and staring them down. Negotiating with a bully is about intimidation and the willingness to confront. In the USA the only person who has the invested power to play that game is the President. His underlings do not have the authority to make threats on the spot. Unless your president knows how to play this game we are at a disadvantage. A recent example is Putin's threats about using nuclear weapons. They should not be taken seriously but we need someone on our side to call his bluff. At this time, we have no leader who has the status and capability to do so. The person who has the status is the President of the USA unfortunately Biden is incapable of playing this role.

Contrastingly Donald Trump grew up in New York making real estate deals, negotiating with City officials, negotiating with unions, negotiating with banks who wanted at times to bankrupt him, negotiating conflicts with contractors. Managing his TV program "the Apprentice" where the famous words were "You're Fired". He has a lot of experience with conflict. Trump likes eyeball to eyeball negotiations. Trump has a very spontaneous, confrontative style. He is not a typical politician. Trump is suited to confronting bullies.

Let's take a look at our 4 THUGS

Vladimir Putin. President of Russia born 1952

Putin worked as a KGB foreign intelligence officer for 16 years, rising to the rank of lieutenant colonel before resigning in 1991 to begin a political career in Saint Petersburg. In 1996, he moved to Moscow to join the administration of President Boris Yeltsin. Putin's moves since then speak of power moves and intrigues that has left him as the autocratic ruler of Russia since 2000.

Xi Jinping born 1953. President People's Republic of China born 1953

Xi is the son of a powerful ally of Chairman Mao, the leader of the Communist revolution. However his father fell out of favor at one point and Xi went from a privileged upbringing to working with peasants for 6 years during the cultural revolution. Since then he has risen through the communist party and was elevated to the role of President in 2013.

Khamenei. Supreme leader of Iran born 1939

Khamenei credentials go way back to when he was exiled by the Shah. Returning after 1979 and the establishment of the religious control of Iran. Became Supreme Leader after the death of Khomeini in 1989.

Kim Jong Un. Born 1982/3

Successor to his father the Great Leader of North Korea. Since his father's death Kim Jong Un has established his position as Supreme Leader of North Korea. North Korea is an oppressive tightly controlled dictatorship.

In reading the above biographies it easy to understand that all of these men have survived and thrived in environments that involved intrigue, assassinations, betrayal. These are all tough cookies who are prepared to take calculated risks in the pursuit of their objectives.

It is also interesting to note that their issues with the test of the world are deeply personal to them.

Vladimir Putin

Putin worked for the KGB for 16 years much of it in East Germany. The challenge in these years was to maintain the Soviet's control over Eastern Europe countries that wanted to be free.

Having been very involved in that struggle one can understand his sense of betrayal when in 1991 it all fell apart with multiple countries choosing to leave the Soviet control and be independent. He has written papers outlining his desire to reconstitute the Soviet Union. In an ironic way one could say that Putin's desire is to "Make Russia Great Again".

The message that we should send to President Putin is as follows:

Dear President Putin,

By trying to takeover Ukraine you are punishing all your current citizens because of the economic hardships and the deaths of their children and fathers. If you succeed in conquering Ukraine all you will have achieved is that you have more disgruntled people that will need your help. We understand that the collapse of the Soviet Union was very personal for you. However, it is gone. Nothing you can do will recreate it.

Conquering Ukraine is a point of pride for you alone. Please find a way out of this mess. If you can be the bigger person you will earn the respect and gratitude of so many people.

Respectfully the world

President Xi Jinping

President Xi's father was a hero in the epic struggle to create the People's Republic of China. His father died in 2002 when President Xi was fifty. It is reasonable to assume that his father helped guide President Xi's rise in the Party. It is also reasonable to assume that the son shared his father's regret that Chiang Kai-Shek escaped to Taiwan with the remnants of his army and set up a competing system of government that has been a success. Taiwan as far as the Revolution is concerned is unfinished business.

The message we should send to President Xi Jinping is as follows:

Dear President Xi,

The revolution that your father helped create is an amazing success. Many challenges lie ahead for the PRC. In an awakening world totalitarian regimes need to evolve in order to sustain the support of their people. Communism had an amazing period of popularity following the second world war but that popularity is fading. Having achieved great economic success what is next for the PRC? It would be a mistake to take on the unfinished business of Taiwan. It is a distraction. You have other more compelling challenges. Let it be.

Respectfully the world

President Khamenei

Here is a message for President Khamenei

Dear President Ali Khamenei,

We understand that your circumstance is very complicated. Since 1979 and the Shah's departure there has been a continuous struggle within Iran between conservative religious leadership and the non-religious hierarchy, more moderate leadership. You are nearly 85 years old. Your country is dug in on opposition to the west and in particular the USA. Saudi Arabia as part of the Abraham Accords has decided to move on and engage with Israel.

Turkey is getting tired of Erdogan and looks like it will turn back once again to the West in two years. What is to be your legacy? You have a choice. You can either die in your current position and let your successors fight it out or you can act now to define the future direction for Iran.

Use your power to advance moderate leaders to positions in the administration.

Expand this network over the next five years. Wait for some event that provides a reason to change policies and declare the war against the Big Satan and the little Satan is over.

I realize that this is asking a lot but I think God would give these initiatives his blessing. The time for Islam to be a "warrior" religion is over. Islam is spreading across the globe on its own merits. Do not punish Islam by trying to kill all the Jews.

Respectfully the world

Supreme Leader Kim Jong Un

Dear Supreme Leader Kim Jong Un,

We understand that your family has ruled N. Korea since 1948. Following the Korean War end in 1953 your country has had only two allies who like yourself are totalitarian societies, China and Russia. It is time to find a path to rejoin the global community. We understand that it is very difficult for you to turn away from the heritage of your grandfather and your father but it is time. Declare your interest in making peace with South Korea and the world will welcome you and your people. It is time to do this.

Respectfully the world

CHAPTER 6

THE HUMAN REALITY

All human activity is based on the zoological and social realities of the human being. Everything can be connected to these underlying factors.

Many intellectuals live in and believe in an international multicultural world of open borders. This is not an imagined environment. It is the one they live in. They travel to international conferences to meet similar colleagues. Such conferences occur in several places in the world every week of the year eg. United Nation Conferences, Global Climate Change Conferences like the one recently held in Dubai, the World Economic Forum held in Davos each year, Academic Conferences, European Conferences, Asian Pacific Cooperation Conference, Business Conferences etc. At such conferences they meet similarly highly educated people from all different cultures who share their concerns and are indeed colleagues. They feel strongly that the global communities all share the same objectives. I used to be part of that global elite flying around the world visiting various operations and customers. What the global elite forget is that the great, great majority of people live and die within fifty miles of where they were born. Let's call these people the local folks in comparison to the global elite. The local folks are the product of their environment and, even if they are limited in their world view, they vote and are entitled to their opinion. The local folks are strongly tribal. As humans we have deep needs to identify with and belong to a tribe.

Whether you are one of the global elite or one of the local folks the only measure of a person is their character. Individuals of good character can exist in both spheres, the global elite and the local folks. I am suspicious of the idea of a shared global culture. It is certainly not achievable in our lifetime. The variety of cultures in the world have value, create debate and consequently progress. The local folks find the idea of an imposed global culture invasive and offensive. We need to respect each other and agree to disagree. I side with the local folks.

In a shrinking world we face many challenges today. Around the world we have a wide array of diverse people all with different cultures and histories. How do we manage to coexist and work together in a harmonious way? We need to connect around something that we share and that is VALUES. What makes a good person is a universal reality. In every society the ingredients that make a good person are the same. The struggle for day-to-day material wellbeing in the West and many other places is essentially over. The struggle to create high value societies based on fundamental human truths is ongoing. We need to build civil societies worth living in. In many parts of society and the world we are lost souls because we lack the values that guide character. The global uniformity I seek is on values.

The Beast Within Us

When the sun comes up on the Serengeti plains the rhythm of another day starts. The gazelles and the zebra start to move to take on water or to graze. They move in herds. They keep an eye open for the leopards in trees and prides of lions relaxing in the shade. The lions meanwhile observe while the young cubs play. Although everything seems peaceful everyone is keeping an eye on the others and trying to maintain safe spacing. The herds grazing on the plains want to be left alone. The lions and leopard want to kill and eat one of the grazing animals. They have to in order to survive. That is nature.

The kill comes suddenly and quickly. The lions see a calf that has lingered a little and just for a moment become a little separated from the herd. The lions suddenly break into a sprint. The herd moves. The young calf desperately tries to regain the safety of the herd. It is too late.

One lion springs on its back and within seconds four more lions arrive tearing at the calf as its heart still beats. The end is quick. That is nature.

Within each of us are the instincts of fight and flight, the instincts to survive when faced with danger. We, like animals, are wary particularly in a strange environment. We understand that if we are at the wrong place at the wrong time we can be hurt, robbed, raped, even killed. It happens every day throughout the world. Some of us grow up in environments where such risks are very common. Others live in environments where they rarely or never are exposed to such threats. However, within each of us are the instincts of fight or flight, embedded within us from our ancestors waiting to be activated by circumstance. The circumstance could be confronting a grizzly bear in the woods. Being caught by a rip tide when swimming. A fight in a bar with strangers. These situations have a biological response which is the triggering of a surge of adrenalin which allows us to fight harder, run faster or in any way possible try to survive the situation. This is an instinct that we share with the gazelle and the lion.

We see ourselves as civilized. We are, but the veneer of civilization is fragile. Individuals and groups of individuals commit horrendous uncivilized acts on an ongoing basis. There are spontaneous acts and institutionalized acts. Spontaneous acts are triggered by some event that triggers the beast within a person or a group and some person is badly beaten or killed.

Institutionalized acts occur when someone in authority orders others to kill. Examples of this are:

- Hitler and the Jews from 1940 to 1945. The Holocaust killed an estimated 6 million Jews which was about 80% of the European population of Jews. If you include others who were killed such as Communists, Jehovah Witnesses, Gypsies, POW's, Free Masons, homosexuals and others the total killed rises to 15 to 20 million.
- The Khmer Rouge led by Pol Pot in Cambodia from 1970 to 1975 killed or worked to death about 3 million Cambodians.
- The Yugoslav Wars following the death of Tito and the breakup of Yugoslavia led to the Serbs killings of Muslim Bosnians from 1992 to 1995 and the systematic rape of the Muslim Albanian minority women in the tens of thousands.
- The killing of the Tutsi by the Hutu in Rwanda in 1994 yielded between 500000 and 1 million deaths in 100 days.

- ISIS in Syria, Iraq and spreading to Libya, Sinai, Sub-Sahara Africa, Yemen and other places is killing many and enslaving others at a pace yet to be accounted.
- Hamas in Gaza slaughtering 1160 Israelis on September 7th 2023.

The noticeable fact is that this institutionalized barbarity continues in recent times with the clear message that the "Beast within Us" can be easily woken.

If Fight or Flight is one of our inherited bestial instincts it is not on display as often as our other bestial instinct: the drive, particularly in males, to have sexual intercourse once aroused. Sexual arousal happens in response to stimuli that can be visual, scent and touch.

Women often accuse men of thinking with their penis instead of their brain. This can occur when a male has been aroused. When a man is thinking only with his penis he is not a lot different from a beast. Men are more easily and quickly aroused than females. It is a fact that most rapes are perpetrated by males, and it is a fact that the female prostitution industry is much larger than the male version. Human males inflict a fair amount of chaos because of their sexual arousal needs. It used to be that in order to be guaranteed regular sex males married. Females understood that and negotiated for marriage as the price for regular sex. Birth control and ready access to abortions have undercut the female platform to be able to negotiate for marriage.

"humans are at their core beasts"

The Antidote to the Beast: Parenting

There are 8 billion persons in the world. Each born into a unique circumstance that will shape who they will become and their future. Although on the outside we are all dramatically different on the inside we all want the same things. Our family circumstance will shape each of us and, for most of us, determine our role in life.

Think of the beast as being a primal source of energy within all of us. Some of us have a lot of it others not so much. However, all of us have some. This energy can result in good or evil. The type of parenting you receive along with the social norms of the society you grow up in will determine what the outcome is. This parenting thing is unfair. You do not get to choose your parents or your place of birth. You do not get to choose your body. It is one big lottery. You may be lucky or unlucky in all these matters that will be so important in your life. The takeaway is that life at its beginning is profoundly unfair. This is a fact worth dwelling upon because there are people who think that this unfairness can somehow be compensated for so that we can get equal outcomes. This is naive. Our responsibility as a society is to provide good educational and training avenues and try our very best to create equal opportunities for those who are motivated to seek them. We can help the disadvantaged and yes a few, because of their individual drive, will rise far above their disadvantaged start. However, most will not. Life is not about equal outcomes it is about how far you have come from where you started. That is how we should measure a person.

In adolescence the child starts to evaluate more critically their circumstance. They start to compare their family and themselves against those of their peers. At this stage all adolescents are unsure of themselves, sometimes terribly so. Each person has been dealt certain cards that they have no control over. However, each person has, starting in adolescence, increasing control of the choices they make. This is what life is all about. This is the start of life for the individual.

You begin to understand the cards you were dealt and consider the choices you have.

"The start of life is profoundly unfair."

Values

You get most of your values from your parents. If your parents are scumbags then your values may be dodgy. Why are values important? Values speak to character and character, in the long term, is everything. In the long term you can only succeed with the cooperation and support of others and that only happens if you have good character. Good character is the right values combined with the self-disciplines that create integrity. The two go together. Having good values but no self-discipline creates a life of remorse or excuses. What is good character has not changed in 2000 years. In these 2000 years everything else has changed but not what is good character.

Good Character = Good Values + Self Discipline

Most of the people in the world, whether they are actively religious or not, are taught values that have a basis in religion. Out of the 8 billion people in the world there are about 2.4 billion Christians 1.9 billion Muslims, 1 billion Hindus and 16 million Jews. 97% of the world population claim some kind of religious affiliation.

Good character is important to inner peace. In life we all screw up from time to time. Nobody lives a perfect life. When we reflect on our own screw-ups, we always need to examine our motivation. If we were trying to do the right thing and it just got messed up, then it is easier to forgive yourself and have inner resolution and possibly peace. However, if we know that our motivations were inconsistent with good character we will not have inner peace even when we are successful. Some people will point to persons who are very successful but of poor character and say "So what?" Such statements beg the question of "What is the purpose of a life." Good persons are individuals with the right values who also have the self-discipline to act consistent with their values. Simply stated, people of good character are good people.

If values create the vessel education fills the vessel. Education to a high level is very, very important not only to the individual but also to creating a civil society. Depending on where you grow up in the world you may receive a lot of education or very little. Education is not just about learning stuff it is also about developing the habits of studying, of thinking and of critical analysis. It is these habits in the individual that lead to progress. It is an abomination that in the US many children do not get a good High School education. The harm that this does to the individual is only eclipsed by the harmful consequences to society.

Tribalism

We all have a tribal identity, perhaps several. Our core tribe is the family in which we are raised. Beyond that there is religion, race, community, State, and a Nation. Then there are sub-tribes, your profession, the company you work for, a political party, a sports team. Most humans have strong needs to belong, so they want the acceptance that comes with these identities.

Tribalism is everywhere. You are white, black, brown or yellow. You are a Christian, Muslim, Jew, Hindu, Buddhist or other. You are British, French, German, Chinese, Japanese or or…there are 195 countries. You are heterosexual or perhaps something else. The stronger the demands of the tribe the stronger the bond. Think of those you know who have been US Marines or Navy Seals. It is a lifetime connection. Most Muslims feel the same way about Islam. The demands are great but the followers welcome being lead.

I could go on and on about how we self-identify and carry suspicions and grudges from the past. It has a lot to do with what our parents transfer to us and how history is taught in schools. If you live in an advanced economy and are well educated then you probably can place history in its proper place, the past. If you are poorer, not educated all you probably have is your tribal identity and an awareness of all the wrongs perpetuated by your neighbors over the last several hundred years. These histories only recede when they are replaced by a better future, the rule of law and a vested interest i.e. a middle class. As a world we have many major impediments to peace and progress because of historical tribal hatred.

"Humanity is a collection of tribes."

Instinctive Stereotyping

Although we view ourselves as very advanced, within us are all the instinctive reactions that any animal has. If an animal is in a forest and hears a noise caused by the movement of another animal, it will pause to assess. If it sees the animal, it will immediately sort it into either an enemy that wants to kill and eat it, a non-threatening like species or a possible source of food.

Depending on the situation further sorting is done immediately. Is it young/old, male/female or strong/weak. These are all the instincts that are associated with self-preservation and self-interest. In today's world humans go through the same instinctive process. Since we are all the same species the sorting is slightly different based on recognizable differences. Every person has their own criteria that they use but they include observable differences (black, white, yellow, brown), young or old, male or female, physically intimidating or not, mode of dress and physical location (country, urban, low crime area, high crime area). Every individual does not have the same rating system but nevertheless they have it based on their personal experience and what they have been taught. Some people call these built in filtering systems prejudices or stereotyping. I would suggest they are human realities and not to have them is reckless. As individuals we can sense the initial reactions in others to ourselves. Now if we have an opportunity to interact with strangers, we quickly get more data in the form of speech, speech content and body language that allows us to further evaluate the person as an individual as opposed to as a member of a group. I think this is just the way it is. Consequently, I have difficulty being outraged by the micro-aggression movement. What is called "bias speech" is individuals inadvertently disclosing their own filtering assumptions about others. Since we all have them to a greater or lesser extent, I think we need to recognize that such stereotyping is a normal and reasonable filtering process. When you get to interact with an individual you should put your filtering assumptions in your back pocket and reassess them based on their individual behavior but is it such a big deal that individuals have these filtering assumptions.

"Be aware of strangers is just not a mother's teaching it is an intuitive tribal response."

The Power of One

Individuals can and do influence the path the world community takes. Ideas that excite the mind and leadership that can harness the energies of many persons define the path we take. This possibility is one of the most exciting things about being alive.

There are 8 billion people in the world. That's a lot of folks. Every year about 61 million people die and every year 134 million are born. So every day about 167000 people die all over the world. The number of people who retire from full time employment every year is approximately the same as those who die…..61 million a year and 167000 a day.

So the challenge the world faces is how do we take the approximately 134 million babies that are born every year and raise them, train them, motivate them to grow up and be ready after appropriate experience to be a good person and capable of filling all the jobs that are vacated by the knock on effect of these 61 million people retiring every year. We also need to create an additional 76 million jobs through economic growth to keep everyone usefully employed.

The effective working career of an individual is about 40 years, say from 25 to 65. The years from 0 to 25 are the formative years and most people do not dramatically change their values, their personality and their life viewpoints after that.

The years 25 to 30 are about starting a career and gaining experience in your field. After 30 some people will play more important roles than others. Some will start businesses. Others will advance to positions of increasing responsibility. Others still will play major roles in their community and family by staying right there and doing a great job every day. To have a civil society worth living in we need good persons at every level in society

The challenge is how do we maximize the number of good persons in each year's newly born class of about 134 million individuals. This seems like a dream challenge for a social scientist and when you pose the problem on this scale it seems to beg the involvement of government in some way. I may surprise you by suggesting that governments have a limited role to play, and I am especially wary of social scientists since it is fairly evident that although there is some real social science there is also a lot of opinions and theories masquerading as science. Instead, I believe in "The Power of One."

By "the Power of One" I am talking about a single individual and since individuals are formed in families, I am willing to extend the term to include families. I believe that civilization has to the greatest extent been moved forward by highly motivated individuals who are good people. Think about how civilization has moved forward over the last 1000 years. The innovations have come from individuals. All great art (Leonardo da Vinci, Michelangelo, Pollock, Picasso, Matisse, Van Gogh, Chagall, Calder, Dali etc.), all scientific discoveries (Einstein, Newton, Aristotle, Fleming, Tesla, Pasteur, Curie, Galileo , Pascal, etc.) all truly great product innovations (Edison, Watt, Jobs, Ford, Graham Bell, Nobel, Benz etc.), all great companies (Rockefeller, Carnegie, Westinghouse , Ford, Gates, Heinz, Tata, Agnelli , Lilly etc.) all medical breakthroughs (Barnard, Cushing, Ehlrich, Freud, Hemlich, Fleming, Lister, Salk etc.) all famous political leaders that made a difference (Winston Churchill, Thomas Jefferson, Nelson Mandela, Deng Xiaoping, Margaret Thatcher, Ronald Reagan etc.) I could go on and on about giving evidence that it is the individual not government that spurs civilization forward, but I think you get the point. Progress comes from "Individual Think" not "Group Think."

The takeaway is that we must create environments that respect the individuality of families and give individuals, particularly highly talented and motivated individuals, every opportunity to thrive and grow. It is the competition between ideas in a marketplace that creates the best outcomes for society overall. The philosopher who best understood this was my fellow Scot Adam Smith in his writing "The Wealth of Nations". Adam Smith expounded the counter intuitive idea that individuals by pursuing their self-interest would benefit society overall. The idea is powerful and is the basis of free market capitalism. In free markets individuals are free to compete and the best person, idea or product wins. Many of course fail. This competition for attention creates innovation and progress. It is all about the Power of One and free markets. What I am describing is a meritocracy. To drive home that fact here are brief profiles of eight people who have played or are playing significant roles in trying to make a positive difference in the world.

Ronald Reagan US President 1981-1989

In the 1980's Ronald Reagan renewed Americans belief in our essential goodness. Remember "the shining city on a hill" speech. At the same time, he built up our defense budget and confronted the Soviet Union directly. Remember his "Mr. Gorbachev tear down this wall' speech in Berlin. The Soviet Union buckled, and the cold war was over. Unfortunately democracy in Russia failed and the thugs took over.

Margaret Thatcher UK Prime Minister 1979-1990

Margaret Thatcher was a key ally of Ronald Reagan in facing down the Soviet Union. She also faced down the trade unions and other socialist trends in the UK. She kept the UK out of the European Union euro currency. She was a fighter who steered her country and the west in a positive direction. She was an outstanding female role model.

Nelson Mandela President of South Africa 1994-1999

Nelson Mandela grew up as a black man in white South Africa. He spent his life in the African National Congress party fighting to overcome the "apartheid" regime. He was found guilty of terrorism and sentenced to life in prison. Released in 1990, he worked with de Klerk to manage the transition to a multiracial society. He became the first President of an integrated South Africa. He came across as a kind and forgiving person and he gave South Africa it's best chance for success. A chance that has been wasted by subsequent ANC leaders.

Elizabeth Queen of England 1952-2022

Elizabeth reigned over a time period when the British Empire was dissolved and when, she was first Queen, many labor MP's thought the UK did not need royalty. She re-established the credibility of the UK's government structure and sustained the British Commonwealth which is an important multi-cultural organization mainly made up of Britain's ex-colonies.

Abdel Fattah el-Sisi President of Egypt 2014-present

Egypt with 114 million citizens is the largest Middle East country. It is a country that has flirted with communism under Nasser and was the birthplace of the Muslim Brotherhood from which most Islam terrorism has emerged. He has kept Egypt at peace and has built a positive relationship with Israel. We all need to be appreciative of this man.

Benjamin Netanyahu Prime Minister of Israel 1996-1999 2009-2021 2022-present

Bibi comes from a family that has dedicated itself to the creation and the survival of Israel. Leading Israel is one of the toughest jobs on the planet.

Muhammad bin Salman. Crown Prince and Prime Minister of Saudi Arabia 2022- present

This man is trying to manage the transition of Saudi Arabia from the most conservative Sunni Muslim country, totally dependent on oil, to a country with relationships with Israel and with a much more diverse modern economy. We should all wish him well.

Volodymyr Zelensky President of Ukraine. 2019-present

Catapulted into prominence when Russia invaded Ukraine in February of 2022. Tirelessly working to solicit the support for this war at the same time managing the internal affairs of Ukraine. Another person to thank.

Donald Trump, ex-President of the USA

Not ideological. Sees the world as a series of practical problems to be solved. Not a globalist. Because of his experience in negotiating deals the best person to confront the four THUGS discussed in Chapter 5. At the age of 78 and very rich dedicating his life to making a difference. A very controversial person but the best measure of him is his children. They all turned out good.

It is scary how much influence these individuals are having in shaping the world we live in. Who we vote for is very important. We always should choose a good person with a proven track record.

"It is good individuals, not groups, that drive progress."

Last thought……what can you do that is important? Strive to be a "good person" and use that power to help your children and other young people to also be "good persons".